MAKE IT
YOUR OWN
LAW FIRM

The Ultimate Law Student's Guide to Owning, Managing, and Marketing Your Own Successful Law Firm

Spencer Marc Aronfeld
Attorney at Law

Foreword by Morris Dees, Founder of the Southern Poverty Law Center

authorHOUSE®

AuthorHouse™
1663 Liberty Drive
Bloomington, IN 47403
www.authorhouse.com
Phone: 1-800-839-8640

Photographer: Pascal Depuhl http://www.depuhl.com
Stylist, Alex Odio, Artigiano Classic Mens Fashion, http://www.artigianomens.com
Public Relations guru, Charles Jones of CJones & Associates PR.

First published by AuthorHouse 3/11/2011

ISBN: 978-1-4567-3314-8 (sc)
ISBN: 978-1-4567-3312-4 (dj)
ISBN: 978-1-4567-3313-1 (e)

Library of Congress Control Number: 2011900800

Printed in the United States of America

PREFACE

This book is for everyone who has ever dreamed of being a lawyer and possesses the passion to represent those who cannot speak for themselves. It is especially intended to offer a path to aspiring lawyers who sacrificed so much and worked so hard to attend and then graduate from law school, passing the Bar only to find no viable opportunity to practice law.

It is my sincere hope that no other law school graduates will ever be faced with the prospect of abandoning their destiny simply because of not having a job offer or accepting a position that they hate because they have no other choice. I hope that this book creates more opportunities for passionate lawyers to start their own law firms, resulting in greater access to legal representation to those members of our community in need.

CONTENTS

FOREWORD

I had the pleasure of meeting Spencer on a hot August morning in 1997 at Gerry Spence's ranch in Wyoming. Spencer, along with 49 other trial lawyers, was sweating in Spence's barn-turned mock trial court room, trying to learn how to be better lawyers. Spencer and I immediately bonded and when I learned that he started his own firm—from scratch right out of law school and with no formal training—I was even more impressed.

Over the years, Spencer and I stayed in touch. When he told me about this book and asked me to write the foreword, I was flattered and proud. I think it this is an important book because it will provide a road map for many young lawyers and recent law school graduates on how to create their own law firms.

Many bright and talented lawyers never have an opportunity to practice law due to an unfriendly job market. Spencer openly and honestly tells how he did it and gives hope and empowerment to a whole new generation of lawyers.

I told Spencer, that I wish I had had a copy of this book when I first started practicing law. Although I had enjoyed a successful business career before law school, this book gives a logical step-by-step approach without any candy coating.

Morris Dees
Founder of the Southern Poverty Law Center
Montgomery, Alabama

ACKNOWLEDGMENTS

My solo flight would not have been possible without the many, many shoulders I have stood upon and continue to stand on every day. It is with most sincere gratitude to all those who supported me that I dedicate this, my first book.

To my grandfather, Samuel Aronfeld, whom I have never met and who passed away long before I was born, but who serves as the honorary founding partner of my firm and whose portrait hangs in my office. To the memory of his wife, my grandmother, Rose Dorothy Aronfeld, who loved me immeasurably. To my father, Norwin Aronfeld, who convinced me to go to law school and who worked hard and sacrificed much in his own life to pay for my education. To my mother and biggest fan, Candace Elias Grossman, who infuses me with the ability to care about people other than myself. In memory of her late husband, Harold Stanley Grossman, who proudly sat through days of my trials and kept me company on the long drives home after many of my losses. To my beautiful wife, Dina, and our children, Sara Rose and Nory, who have somehow tolerated my exhaustion and crankiness when I am home and my absence when I am on the road. To the Flying Mendez Brothers, Ignacio and Armando; my life's best friend, Donald Elliot Baker; the late Myles J. Tralins, Esquire, who fired me and told me to go it alone; and the late, great Jon H. Daughtery, one of my first clients, a dear friend and teacher, and the best lawyer to ever practice without a license; Marco Rojas, for referring me the Disney case that changed my life; Marc Michelson, Esquire, who taught me so much; Samy Chong, who taught me to accept myself. To the brilliant, late Patrice Talisman, Esquire, for without her love and counsel, I would most certainly be homeless or working at Starbucks. To Kenneth J. Bush, Esquire, who has gently taught me and guided me through the minefield of practicing law by answering my questions both day and night. Kenny has never asked me for anything in exchange for the thousands of hours he has given to sculpt me into the lawyer that I am today.

Thank you to all the people who have worked with me in the office over the years, especially those who are there now and have allowed me the time to write this book. In particular each word that you read, every comma, period and hyphen was lovingly edited by my talented friend and editor, Bruce E. Shemrock, Esquire.

I also must thank each and every client who has trusted me, for better or worse, to be his or her voice.

And, lastly and perhaps most significantly, to the great Gerry L. Spence, who is not just the best lawyer in history, but a wonderful teacher and friend. It is in his honor and in honor of all those who have helped me that I feel compelled to pass on whatever knowledge I have acquired to the next generation.

WHY I WROTE THIS BOOK

I have owned and operated my own law firm from the day I was sworn in as a lawyer. Not because I wanted to or because it was my dream, but because even though I graduated from the University of Miami School of Law, *cum laude,* in 1991, I simply could not get an interview, much less a job.

Since 1991, I have been my own boss, handling my own cases, employees, and business. I currently have an associate and five employees. I have handled cases in many states, am board certified by the Florida Bar in Civil Trial,[1] and my firm is AV rated by Martindale Hubbell. Board certification recognizes attorneys who have special knowledge, skills, and proficiency in various areas of law and professionalism and ethics in practice.

In this book, I will share with you a clear recipe for how you too can start your own law firm right out of law school. Hopefully, you will find having your own law practice as rewarding and fulfilling as I have. And remember, when it's your firm, you cannot be fired or laid off.

---

1   Certification is the highest level of evaluation by the Florida Bar of the competency and experience of attorneys. There are twenty-four areas of law approved for certification by the Supreme Court of Florida. Board-certified Florida Bar members are the only Florida attorneys allowed to identify themselves as "Specialist" or "Expert" or to use the letters "B.C.S." on business cards or letterheads.

ABOUT ME

So that you do not think I am special or any different from you, let me share a little about how I ended up where I am. I went to law school in large part because my father, whose father was a lawyer, was convinced that it would not only be a great education for me, but it would also provide the foundation for an excellent career. I believe that my dad never actually envisioned that I would be a practicing lawyer but rather a businessman who had a law license.

I was convinced that I was intellectually unqualified for law school, having been intimidated as an undergraduate by the law students on campus. They carried around such big books and always seemed so stressed out and serious. I would see them scurrying to the library after inhaling dinner in the cafeteria, while I hung around for hours with nothing to do but go back to my dorm room and sleep.

The LSAT was no picnic for me, either. My pretests seem to be a constant negative predictor that I was not smart enough to be a law student, much less a lawyer. Studying for the multiple-choice test of reading comprehension and logic further convinced me that my dad had no idea what he was talking about. My median-level score reaffirmed this by telling me that I was just average and was going to be an average law student at an average law school and would become, at best, an average lawyer. How wrong they all were.

I found out that I did not just like law school—I loved it. I was the rare law student who really enjoyed the work. Having suffered horribly in all math, statistics, and accounting classes I had taken, I enjoyed the reading, writing, and thinking that law school involved. I also liked the debating; I enjoyed thinking on my feet and was not afraid to raise my hand and challenge the professors. I thought that for the first—and perhaps only—time in my life, my father was actually right about me.

What surprised me was that after all my success in law school and all of the hard work, I was completely unprepared to practice law as a lawyer. I literally—don't laugh—had no idea where the courthouse was.

I recall one day asking a beloved professor of mine, Alan Swan (who, I am sad to say, died in a car accident in June 2009), what kind of law I should practice. He asked me what I wanted to do, and I said I thought I would like to help hurt people fight the big companies responsible for their injuries. This was based upon my first-year moot court fact pattern, in which a man who had contracted AIDS had sued a condom company for making a defective condom. (That had been my first personal injury case.) Professor Swan laughed in a deep, baritone voice and said that would make me an "ambulance chaser." I had never heard that expression before, but I could tell by the tone of his voice that it must be the lowest species in the lawyer animal kingdom.

As a first-year law student, getting any job, much less a paying job, in the legal field was saved for those precious few who were being groomed by large, fancy law firms to be associates and those with family connections. I had neither.

I finally found a position as a voluntary (unpaid) intern at the Third District Court of Appeal. Even that position was not easy to get and required two interviews and some begging. It was tantamount to spending the summer in the law library of a prison. I was all alone, out in the middle of nowhere off the Florida Turnpike, and I hated it.

These were the only summers in my life that I spent hoping they would end so that school would resume. But at least I had experience that I could put on my resume, although I figured it would ultimately impress few of the people who ever interviewed me for jobs (if anyone). My summer experience clerking did nothing to prepare me to ultimately start my own law firm.

My second summer of law school was the complete opposite from that of my best friend, Donald. The law firms in New York that wanted Donald to come and be a summer associate with them wined, dined, and romanced him like he was a supermodel and they were millionaires. They sent plane tickets and limousines and put him up at five-star hotels. I spent my time signing up for on-campus interviews, but I was rarely chosen for them. I sent out resume after resume and poured over the job postings in the career planning and placement center. Jobs were hard, if not impossible, to come by. Postings were often taken down or hidden by other students to eliminate competition. Eventually, I even considered the dreaded summer school, as I literally had no options. In those days, the University of Miami did not have the summer abroad programs it now offers. I can only assume that these programs serve to occupy the many out-of-work students.

One day (I believe it was the last day of the school year), I was in Donald's *Law Review* office when I saw a job posting on their bulletin board. At the time, I was on the *Inter-American Law Review*, which at the time was considered to be a minor league publication compared to the real *Law Review*.

The job posting was for a law firm on Biscayne Boulevard, in an area that could only flatteringly be described as "the ghetto." I had never heard of the firm—and neither had Martindale-Hubbell, my professors, nor anyone else I asked. But I called and said it was in reference to their posting on the *Law Review*'s bulletin board. (I could not have ever stated that I was actually *on* the *Law Review*, since I was not, just that I saw their posting there).

They invited me for an interview. I think since everybody who was anybody already had a job, and I was willing to work literally for free (though this was to be paid work), I was offered the job. The firm had secretaries, a conference room, computers, and a law library. I still had no idea what a lawyer really did, even though I had already completed two-thirds of my legal education. It was really my first exposure to the practice of law, real lawyers, and a law firm.

At this firm, which shared a floor with the offices of a notorious rapper, I learned a few things—first, that the office manager seemed to be something similar to a prison warden. She frightened the secretaries, swooned around the lawyers, and immediately did not get along with me. In retrospect, I can see that this is a phenomenon I have witnessed with all but one of my own law clerks in subsequent years. The secretaries, for the most part, are younger and less educated than the law clerks. The secretaries are usually hardworking single mothers, and law clerks are usually privileged rich kids who have never had jobs, much less had to work to support anyone.

My lawyers were never there. I think I met one partner once, on the date of the interview; the other, maybe twice. I spent my summer doing busywork, like copying cases out of books or trying to organize files—things that the secretaries would normally do but that they could now bill clients for. I am sure I added little to no actual value to anything that I did that summer. I probably made things worse.

I was also distracted by an ailing grandmother, a broken heart, and sheer loneliness and boredom. There were no other law clerks in the firm, the building, or probably within ten miles. I was not impressed with the locale of the firm, and I am sure they were disappointed in me.

The highlight of that summer came during what can only be summed up as the "popcorn incident," an event my mother has reminded me of frequently throughout my career. I brought a popcorn machine to the office one day—not one of those things on wheels you see in a movie theatre lobby, but a countertop hot air popper. It may have been the only thing I did that summer that the lawyers and secretaries liked. I would make popcorn and put it in Dixie cups and pass the cups around like someone serving tea to tourists at a Turkish rug merchant's shop.

The office manager, an enormous woman in her late twenties, got wind of my popcorn-making hi-jinks, literally, when the smell of fresh popcorn started to compete with and beat whatever smell-seniority her perfume commanded in the office. She went, without any exaggeration, ballistic. I sadly and regrettably made the mistake of confronting her on her objection to my culinary masterpiece. She called the partner who was on his vacation—I am sure with the express intention of getting his permission to fire me. He was either unavailable or unimpressed, and, sadly for her and probably for me too, he did not green-light my pink slip. Instead, we were forced to work together, but never did a kernel pop again in that office—at least not that summer.

A kernel of another kind did pop that summer, and until I began writing this book, that fact never really dawned on me. My mom told me in the midst of my battle with the office manager, "When you have your own firm, you can pop all the popcorn you want." Somewhere in my subconscious mind, the thought of having my own firm was born.

Near the end of my third year, I got another interview with a downtown lawyer named Myles Tralins. Myles was a sole practitioner and at least had an incredible office in a beautiful building, and he hired me on the spot.

Myles Tralins was unlike any lawyer I had ever seen on television. He worked bizarre hours, often starting the day around 5:00 PM and working past 2:00 AM. He could handle any kind of case from, as he would tell me, "administrative law to zoning."

He had an amazing ability to speak, read, and write the law. He was a friend of judges. He could handle a parking ticket in the morning and then try a complicated trademark case that afternoon in front of a jury. He owned airplanes and yachts. His wife was beautiful. His house was filled with real food and great wine. He had an amazing smile, and I loved him.

He also was constantly upset at his staff and at me. Most of us could not satisfy or keep up with him. There were new secretaries every week; many people left crying. Having grown up with an insatiable, demanding father, I could take it. However, somewhere not too deep in both Myles' heart and my own, we knew our professional time together would not be long. I just knew, perhaps better than he did, that I could withstand a higher degree of pain than his average associate or secretary. And like a bicycle race, I might get dropped, but I would never quit.

Eventually, within a week of me getting sworn in as a lawyer, he let me go. We were both relieved. His parting words to me, however, were that I could always "hang out my own shingle." I had no idea what that meant and had never heard that expression. In fact, I thought he was referring to some kind dermatological disorder. Instead, what Myles Tralins was telling me is what I am going to attempt to tell you in this book: *you can always hang out your own shingle.* Read this book, and I will tell you how.

1 Solo Practice:
DO I HAVE THE RIGHT STUFF?

Contrary to the advice of my editor, I am going to give you the number-one secret to success as a solo practitioner right here in the first paragraph of the first chapter. Once you know this secret, you might simply close the book and never buy it. But, here it is, and it's free: *you have to really, really, really want to be a lawyer.*

Most people I know went to law school because they could. They had the brains, the money, the time, no other option, no easier option, or were bored at their first jobs as teachers, accountants, or doctors. Few people I knew in law school, if anyone, had the foresight to know what exactly they were working so hard to become. Ask yourself the following questions and rate your score on a scale of 1–10; 1 = Don't Agree and 10 = Totally Agree:

1. I like to help people. _____

2. I like to spend hours reading. _____

3. I like to work in a very stressful environment. _____

4. I am willing to work night and day and weekends and holidays. _____

5. I like to be in contentious and adversarial relationships with people. _____

6. I like to work under deadlines. _____

7. I like to multitask. _____

8. I like to win. _____

9. I can handle losing without losing it. _____

10. I like to follow rules, even those I do not agree with. _____

While these ten questions are by no means an exhaustive list, I can assure you that there is probably not a law school in the country that has these questions on its application. If there is, please let me know. One reason for this is that the people who make the decision as to who should attend law school have never been lawyers, or they practiced so long ago that whatever they once knew has been erased by time and the reserved parking spaces given to law school administrators.

Let's take a minute to consider just the first statement. "I like to help people" might seem like a no-brainer and an obvious yes. Really, Spencer, how could you even ask such a dumb and obvious question? Okay, let's see how dumb it is. Get your pencil out and fill in the blanks below:

I have demonstrated that I like to help people in the following three ways in the last year:

1. I have _____
    _____.

2. I have _____
    _____.

3. I have _____
    _____.

If you are struggling to complete just the first sentence honestly, then consider this: you can still be a lawyer and make a living—maybe even a great one and one far more lucrative than my own—but will you be happy?

Rosa Romero was my secretary for almost six years. I learned a lot from this lady, who had only a high school diploma and no legal skills when I hired her. She told me often, as I complained about this or that, that for me, being a lawyer was never really "work" since I loved doing it. And she was right. So if you are looking for work or a job or a get-rich-quick scheme, close this book now. I will not be offended. (In fact, I won't even know!)

I say this in seminars I give and see people squirm in their seats. I have seen them close their laptops and walk out. They are doing themselves and their clients a favor. If you were a client, would you rather have a lawyer who was brilliant but hated being a lawyer and did not care for you, or a lawyer with average smarts who loved being a lawyer and really cared for you?

Why does caring for people matter so much, anyway? What if you care only about money or watches or cars? If you care only about money or cars, you should be in the business of business, not the business of providing a legal service to people. For me, that is what being a lawyer has always meant. Being a lawyer means trying to help people who cannot help themselves for whatever reason. My practice has been limited almost from Day One to helping the injured (or those who at least thought or convinced me that they were injured). Most of my clients in Miami do not speak English, have little or no formal education, and just happened to be in the wrong place (at least, as far as I was concerned) at the wrong time.

The same applies to those charged with a crime, going through a divorce, or filing for bankruptcy. These people need to be cared for.

So you want to be a lawyer? There are many different types of attorneys. Do you know what type you want to be? First, do your homework. How many lawyers do you know, and what do they do? Answer the following questions:

I know a lawyer named _____ who practices _____ law.

I like/dislike this lawyer and do/do not want to live like him/her. (Circle as appropriate.)

Keep answering this question until you find a lawyer whose practice suits you.

I guess I was lucky that I found my calling, but many are not. The streets are lined with unhappy and unemployed law school graduates, and the towers of offices in our cities are filled with lawyers who feel stuck in their jobs. Once you have dependents like a spouse, partner, kids, and parents, the ability to get yourself out of your mistaken career choice is even harder, if not impossible.

This is your first case: figure out in which area of practice you want to work. If you have no idea, answer the following questions with either yes or no:

1. I would prefer to spend my day in the courtroom in front of a judge and jury battling it out. _____

2. I would prefer to spend my day in the library, never seeing anyone but doing a lot of research and writing. _____

3. I would prefer to spend my day helping people who make and build things. _____

4. I would prefer to spend my day crunching numbers. I like math. _____

5. I need a nine-to-five job and have other things to do with my time. _____

6. I like law and order and would like more people to just follow the rules. _____

7. I have a strong background in finance and accounting.
   _____

8. I have no idea what I like or what kind of lawyer I want to be.
   _____

9. I want to do it all and would get bored doing just one kind of law. _____

Here is a brief list of the areas of practice that are out there (in no particular order):

1. Criminal defense—the representation of those accused of a crime.

2. Criminal prosecution—the representation of the government enforcing the violation of a criminal law.

3. Family law—the representation of individuals seeking divorce, child custody, or adoption.

4. Bankruptcy law—the representation of corporate or individual debtors or creditors.

5. Immigration law—the representation of individuals seeking to live or work in the United States or defending their deportation or corporations seeking to employ a foreign employee.

6. Personal injury law—the representation of plaintiff (the alleged injured party) and defendant (the alleged responsible party) in accidents, defective products, and medical malpractice.

7. Intellectual property law—the representation of individuals or corporations seeking protection of ideas, patents, and trademarks.

8. Bioethics law—the representation of individuals or corporations in the development and use of pharmaceuticals, medical devices, and procedures.

9. Environmental law—representation of individuals and

corporations responding to or defending natural or manmade disasters or compliance with governmental mandates.

10. Appellate law—representation of individuals, corporations, or governments seeking a review of lower court rulings and findings.

11. Governmental law—working on behalf of the state or federal government for governmental entities such as the Securities and Exchange Commission, the Internal Revenue Service, or Homeland Security.

12. Sports and entertainment law—the representation of individuals and corporations in the areas of sports, music, theater, fashion, and the arts.

The list goes on, and within this list are many specialties and subspecialties.

So here's the plan: Open up your computer and Google the terms, find out who the players (not advertisers) are in your community, and make a list. The list should contain the following information:

Name:
Specialty:
Source:
Address:
E-mail Address:
Phone Number:
Date of Contact:
Docket Date for Response to Contact:
Follow Up:
Follow Up:
Meeting:
Thank You:
Follow Up:

After you have compiled your list, contact the career planning and placement director at a nearby law school. (Start with your local one, even if it is not your law school of choice.) Contact the bar association for your state. Make sure it is the bar association and not one of the voluntary membership clubs that each state, city, and ethnic group has. Most states have a board certification distinction. These are usually given to those lawyers who have demonstrated some kind of distinction and honor in their specialties. Here is a partial list of links to many of the preeminent organizations:

American Bar Association: www.abanet.org
The American Association for Justice: www.justice.org
The American Trial Lawyers Association: www.theatla.com
National Bar Association: www.nationalbar.org
National Board of Legal Specialty Certification: www.nblc.us
Aronfeld Trial Lawyers: www.aronfeld.com

Then look for the national organizations for each legal specialty. You might try contacting the American Bar Association. (In the interest of full disclosure, I will tell you that I joined the ABA in 2009 and attended my very first annual convention.) For personal injury lawyers, the preeminent group is called the American Association for Justice. Each state has a local representative or someone you can contact in the membership office.

Download the events calendars for these organizations. Many of the events are open to the public, or you can simply pay a minimal charge to attend. Find out if you like hanging out with lawyers in one group more than in others. Most lawyers, like most people, seem to fit into similar groups. Tax lawyers seem to be a certain way, just as environmental lawyers tend to be similar to each other in other ways.

I really do not like socializing with lawyers, especially (for the most part) plaintiff's personal injury lawyers. They seem to be very egocentric and competitive. These are two traits that are without a doubt valuable to our craft, but I often feel like I am swimming in a small pool with a lot of sharks. Naturally, that makes me uncomfortable.

You might also try checking out the local bar lunch or cocktail hour. You can often find these listed in the business section of your local paper or the bar news for your state, or just ask your newfound lawyer friends.

Now that you have the list, you will probably see that some names pop up more often than others. Isolate those names and send a letter or e-mail like the one below. (Helpful hint: lawyers have huge egos.)

Dear Lawyer Smith:

My name is Aspiring Lawyer Jones. I have a strong desire to become a lawyer. In researching the different areas of practice and those who are leaders in those areas with the State Bar, Law School, and National Association, I repeatedly came across your name.

I have read with fascination about your career and your cases. I would be greatly honored if I could meet you. I promise I will take no more than ten minutes of your time, as I know and greatly appreciate how valuable your time is.

I am available any morning before 11:00 AM or any afternoon after 4:00 PM. I would like to come to your office and meet you in person. However, if that is impossible, perhaps we could just speak on the phone. [Give options and remember this person is doing you a tremendous favor.]

If there is a person with whom you would prefer I coordinate, please let me know. My phone number is 305-555-5555, and my e-mail address is aspiring@gmail.com.

With sincere appreciation,
Aspiring Lawyer Jones

I also suggest that you spend the five dollars to have some very simple and professional business cards made which clearly display your name and a permanent e-mail address. Many of you reading this book have e-mail accounts at your college or law school that you will most likely lose or abandon upon graduation. Use an e-mail account that you can keep forever, and make sure that it is a very professional name.

Here is a sample:

Aspiring Young Lawyer
aspiring@gmail.com

I have inserted an example of my own business card here.

FRONT

REVERSE

I change my card colors or layout on occasion, but you will note that they are oversized, contain a logo, and have a short list of what I do on the backside in both English and Spanish. Allow me to explain:

1. The oversized card is a conversation starter and will inevitably distinguish your card from the thirty other cards the other lawyer or recipient receives in a given day or week.

2. The logo also differentiates me from the herd of other personal injury lawyers out there, though it is far more common now than when I first start using it in 1996. I strongly urge you to hire a skilled graphic artist and design a logo that will be your trademark and brand. Select something that is unique, legible, and professional. Try several different logos and show them to friends, strangers, and loved ones. Ask them, based upon the logo itself, which they would most likely hire as a lawyer. And for god's sake, please do not select a logo with your three initials—it will look not only like many other lawyers but like the monogram on a pair of Brooks Brothers cufflinks. Unless, of course, you like that kind of thing.

3. The backsides of business cards are valuable and often wasted space. If you are already a lawyer, print there what kind of cases you handle and if you speak another language. Remember that the name of the game is to differentiate your face, firm, and card from the herd.

If you change your cell phone number often, do not include it; simply handwrite the current number on the back of the card. That sometimes will make a potential client feel special. If your cell phone number will remain the same, print it on the cards. These cards can be made at any print store or online. Do not state or imply that you are a lawyer. Do not put flowers or kitty cats on the cards. Opt for off-white paper with simple, clean, legible fonts.

While you are at it, buy some nice paper to use for your thank-you letters (do not spend the money on the preprinted kind) and their envelopes. I suggest that you mail *and* e-mail the letter, as either or both may never make it into the hands of the lawyer.

At this point, you should go back to your contact list and write the date you sent the letter and docket. (See? You are learning legal terms just reading this book!) Follow up with this person within five days. If you find this kind of effort either tedious or risky, you may not want to be a lawyer. After all, you are your first client right now, and your first case is to find out if you want to be a lawyer.

Now, here is what is probably going to happen: You will likely get one of three responses. One response is no response at all. Welcome to the practice of law. Sometimes lawyers simply will not respond. He never got the letter, or whoever filters his mail delivery thought your letter was some kind of junk mail or job application and threw it away (out of service to the lawyer or to protect that person's position in the firm from someone so bright and passionate about being a lawyer that they would write such a letter!).

The second possibility is that the lawyer receives your letter, and it sits on his or her desk amongst the hundreds of pages of stuff the busy lawyer intends to read whenever he or she has a chance—but never does. Eventually, months or years later, this lawyer will get to it and out of sheer embarrassment for not having responded or after never hearing back from you, he or she will throw it out with the old catalogs and seminar flyers.

The third possibility is that you will actually get a call. Now what?

You need to be organized in this process. For those of you who are like I was, fresh out of law school, it may very well be the first time in your life that you have made appointments with professionals for anything other than getting your teeth cleaned. There are a lot of computer programs that can help you keep these appointments, contacts, and notes organized. Most phones have calendars, reminder functions, and contact-management software. To me, it does not matter what you use as long as you use *something* to keep this stuff organized and keep you on time. It may be better to simply buy an agenda at the drug store for five dollars, but you need to keep this stuff accurate.

So, the lawyer calls you—or, more likely, his assistant does. He will say, "We received your letter, and so-and-so lawyer can see you for ten minutes on April 23, 2009." Do not be offended or disappointed if the lawyer gives you an appointment that seems far off. Most lawyers fill their calendars weeks and months in advance. Also, things change, sometimes suddenly, for lawyers. On Monday morning, they may expect the afternoon to go a certain way, only to find out by lunchtime that the day looks completely different than it did at breakfast.

You must be prepared for the meeting. First, you must look presentable and not fashionable. Think Brooks Brothers—not Sean John. Get a haircut, have your nails done, and shave. (Thanks, Mom.)

Be on time and prepared. This sounds like a no-brainer, too—but think about it. You are probably used to arriving to meet friends on "friend time" or getting to class around the time the class started. I certainly was. "Lawyer time" is different from any other time I have ever seen: 9:00 AM means 9:00 AM and not a minute after. *Do not be late.*

Some buildings have tricky and expensive parking situations. Elevators can take forever or only reach certain floors. The addresses listed on some lawyers' websites or business cards are sometimes on different floors than their actual offices. You can and will get lost. If at all possible, make a dry run so you know exactly where the office is and how long it takes to get there.

Plan to arrive at least thirty minutes early. The time spent in the reception area of the lawyer's office is almost as important as the ten minutes you will get with the lawyer. Browse through the magazines that he reads; jot the names down—*Florida Bar News, Field and Stream, Trial,* whatever. Listen to the receptionist. What kinds of calls does it seem she is getting? Does she seem harried and annoyed, or is there a sense of calm elegance to the place?

Who is sitting in the reception area with you? Are they dressed nicely? Do they look like they just robbed a bank? (They may have!) Once I was sitting in a reception area, and I wrongly assumed that the other person waiting was there for a job interview himself. It turned out he was the prime minister of Jamaica. Do not judge a book by its cover.

Regardless of whom the people in the office are or what they look like, the idea for you is to figure out whether you like it and feel comfortable. It may be so fancy and cold and quiet that you are not happy there. Listen to your instincts and take notes.

1. Did the lawyer respond to my invite?

2. If so, was the lawyer open to meeting me, or was he or she snobby about it?

3. How was I greeted when I came to the office? Like a guest? Or like an intruder or a nuisance?

4. How long did I wait to meet the lawyer? Minutes, hours, or less?

Be very nice to the receptionists or assistants. Introduce yourself, get their names, and give each of them one of your cards. Make a note about each person.

Once in the lawyer's office, look around. What kinds of things are important enough to him that he has them in his office? Is there a surfboard? Are there boxing gloves or photos of jazz greats? These are hints that you need to note.

Have a prepared list of questions so you do not waste anyone's time, especially with small talk, unless the lawyer seems to be in no hurry. Some may not be; some may be so flattered by your letter and may love hearing themselves speak so much that you will have much more than ten minutes with them. In fact, you may at some point wish it *were* only ten minutes, so have a backup plan that gets you out the door in case you get caught up in an epic war story all about how brilliant your new hero is.

The list of questions you should focus on is below. You may not get them all answered, and they may not all apply to you, but try to at least get through a few.

1. Why did you become a lawyer?
2. Why do you practice this kind of law?
3. What is a typical day like for you?
4. What kinds of things do you do in your off time?
5. What is the most difficult challenge you have being a lawyer?
6. What advice do you have for me as an aspiring lawyer?
7. What area of the law do you recommend? Why?
8. What area of the law do you not recommend? Why?
9. Would you do it again?
10. Can I watch you work?

Number ten is by far the most important question I can suggest you get an answer to since these lawyers can say whatever they want about their lives. When you are listening to them speak, you can imagine that what they are saying is accurate—but maybe it is not. Seeing, smelling, and feeling it, however, are distinctly different from just hearing about it.

For instance, if you are meeting with a criminal defense lawyer and she amazes you by talking about the exciting preliminary arraignments she goes to every morning, ask if you can go too. Find out what it's like to have to park at the criminal courthouse, take an elevator, wait (sometimes hours) to be heard for a few minutes, and then run to your next hearing down the hall or across town.

Take notes, and do not be late. *Do not be late.* Do not be a hassle. Do not ask too many questions or distract the lawyer—"Why are you doing this? Why are you not doing that?"—unless given the opportunity. Just watch and listen and feel. Throughout, think about whether you like this.

If the lawyer is done and you are alone in the courthouse, take the opportunity to walk around. Go to the clerk's office or the law library. Look into other courtrooms and watch what is happening.

You could and should even go into a judge's chambers and speak to an assistant. Get the judge's info or, even better, if the assistant appears not to be too busy, introduce yourself and give him or her your card. Ask if you can meet with the judge for ten minutes sometime soon. Let the assistant know you are not a party to any case that the judge has. Most judges are elected officials, and while they are often holier than thou, they are still politicians who need to be reelected. Make notes.

Below are ten questions for you to ask your new friend, the judge. Remember that judges were once law students and lawyers themselves.

1. Why did you become a lawyer?

2. What kind of law did you practice when you were a lawyer?

3. Why and when did you become a judge?

4. What is the most rewarding part of being a judge?

5. What is the most challenging part of being a judge?

6. What do lawyers do that you find most disturbing?

7. What do lawyers do that you find most impressive?

8. What lawyers do you suggest I meet to discuss my passion to be a lawyer?

9. What advice can you give me?

10. Can I watch you in court one day?

Once you have the answers (or at least some of the answers) to these questions, make sure that you record them in your database.

Each encounter must be followed up with a thank-you letter. I have horrible and embarrassing penmanship; so, unless you (unlike me) can handwrite something beautifully, send a typed letter like this one:

> Dear Lawyer/Judge:
>
> Thank you for meeting me. I appreciate your generosity and candor. I hope that I will have the privilege of meeting you again.
>
> With respect,
> Aspiring Young Lawyer

You have to send this letter even if you think that your time with this lawyer or judge was a complete disaster. You never know how or when you will see this person again. She could be a judge on one of your cases, an opposing counsel on a case, a mentor, or a referral source years later when you hang your own shingle. Stay in touch and follow up. Depending on the nature of your meeting, I suggest you follow up with a periodic update. Contact them when you get admitted to law school or when you graduate, publish something, or do anything that may in any way give you a reason to send a note.

You should also be on the lookout for things that this particular lawyer might do. Google News can be set up to alert you when a particular name appears in an online publication; use this feature to track when the lawyers you met with appear in news stories.

Networking, cultivating, marketing, follow-up, organization— welcome to being a lawyer. This research may seem time-consuming and expensive. It is. But I assure you that the time spent doing this now will be far less than the tuition and time you will spend becoming a lawyer only to get these invaluable insight years later.

I suggest you go through this process for several lawyers in several areas of law. If, after all this, you come away convinced that you still want to be a lawyer but are undecided on what area of specialty to focus on, read on.

INDEPENDENCE

Let's just take a minute to reflect on the kind of research, attitude, and passion that it takes to do what I suggested above. Was it fun, interesting, lonely, boring, and exciting—or did you think it was a waste of time? If it was anything but thrilling, I would suggest that you are already showing some signs that being a lawyer is not for you. That is okay. You can close the book now. You may actually thank me later.

As time consuming as this exercise is, it is also accurate. It requires you to do research, put yourself out there, withstand rejection, make contacts, be on time, and get your tush off the couch and into a suit. Welcome to the practice of law. If you did it correctly, you probably waited around a lot. You might have been stood up or even laughed at. Perfect: that is a typical day for most lawyers.

But were you lonely? Did you feel that you needed to have co-workers, classmates, or teammates around you? I can understand, but it's lonely at the top, middle, and bottom of having your own law firm. Get used to the pain or pleasure of it. If you are going to be your own boss, you are usually flying solo: alone in the cockpit—no flight attendants, no passengers, and no co-pilot.

DESPERATION

I was desperate to start my own law practice, quite frankly, because I had no other visible or viable options, but maybe you do. Maybe you have a job offer or a position and do not have to go through all this drama. Maybe you are one of the lucky ones who have options and just might not have ever considered having your own law firm as a legitimate choice.

My advice? Take the option of working for someone else, even if the goal is solo practice. You might be asking yourself, *"What? Then why even read this book?"* Here's my thought: law school barely taught me enough to pass the bar, much less where the courthouse is. But if someone else is willing to pay you to learn those things, take them up on it—but first read my chapter on working for someone else.

Be careful about where and with whom you start your career since you will be associated with that person, firm, or area of practice for good or bad, no matter what happens afterward. You also need to learn from the best—or at least the best you can access. So, doing some of the research, interviews, and hoofing it that I suggest above, at a minimum, will help you make a better choice about with whom you should ultimately accept your first job.

Many of my friends, maybe out of desperation and probably out of a simple lack of knowledge, accepted jobs doing the wrong stuff with the wrong firms—at least the wrong firms for them. They started doing the work and *hated* it, cursing the days spent in law school, their bosses, their clients, and themselves.

The other option is to do both. That is, find a place that will allow you to work for them *and* cultivate your own practice at the same time. There are many such opportunities out there where lawyers can take on their own clients on their own time. (Always have this understood and agreed upon *in writing* before you start working with your employer.)

GOLDEN RULE: FOCUS AND COMMIT.

My ultimate recommendation comes from a lifetime spent completely out of balance. I like and function best when I do something to its extreme without distraction. For instance, I am writing this book by sitting in a hotel in Las Vegas, away from my family and my office, and with no distractions (I do not drink, smoke, or gamble). My Blackberry is off, and my e-mail alert is disabled. Why? Because I cannot work on more than one thing at one time. My point is this: if you are going to start your own law firm, commit yourself fully to the process and do not be distracted by serving as a slave to any other master than yourself.

Read on!

2 Leaving the Nest:
FLYING SOLO FROM AN EXISTING JOB

People who have jobs with nice law firms (but somehow think the grass would be greener if their names were on the letterhead) often ask me whether they should leave their employers. I have never really worked for a law firm, but I sure know what it is like to be on my own.

Do you work for a law firm? Is someone paying you a salary, providing you with support staff, parking, and insurance, as well as financing your cases, your bar dues, and the toilet paper in the bathroom? If so, I urge you to think twice before leaving that support. Consider the following:

You can open your own law firm while working on someone else's dime. You may even be far more valuable to the firm than either you or your employer realizes. If you are an associate or partner in a law firm for any length of time and still have your job, chances are you are not only making money for yourself but for your law firm as well. (I am assuming that if you were not profitable for the firm, they would have let you go long ago.)

Your firm, I assume, has also spent a lot of time and money training you and would have to spend even more finding a replacement for you and training him or her. Most importantly, I assume they trust you and you like them. If none of my foregoing assumptions are accurate for your present job, please skip this chapter and go on to the next. If you are not sure, complete or note your agreement/disagreement with the following statements:

1. If I leave, I will make _____ money.
2. If I leave, I will have _____ independence.
3. If I leave, I will have _____ control over case/client selection.
4. If I leave, I will have _____ overhead.
5. If I leave, I will have _____ distractions.
6. If I leave, I will have _____ stress.
7. If I leave, I will have _____ name recognition.
8. If I leave, I will have _____ HR headaches.
9. If I leave I will have _____ sleepless nights.
10. If I leave, my life will be _____.
11. I have been at this firm for _____ years.
12. I am currently practicing in the area of my choice. _____.
13. I like the people I work with. _____.
14. I like the location of the office. _____.
15. I like and respect my employer. _____.
16. I am proud to say I work at this firm. _____.
17. I make $_____ a year now but would like to make $_____.
18. I have the ability to attract and keep clients myself. _____.
19. I have the desire to attract and keep clients myself. _____.
20. I have administrative duties now, enjoy them, and would like more. _____

Many lawyers I meet who work in large firms really only know lawyers who work in large firms. They have no more of an idea what solo practice is than most law school graduates know about the practice of law. Some of them are amazed when I tell them I have to change the toilet paper rolls in my office regularly, decide the color of the paint in the reception area, or design my firm's website. There are thousands of things the sole practitioner has to do that the large-firm lawyer has never considered; it is as if some magical elf goes into their offices at night to make sure that there are printer toner cartridges in the copy machine.

If you are thinking about opening your own law firm, before you make the leap, you must meet and speak with some lawyers who have their own firms, specifically those who practice in the area you are considering. Go see their offices, do some due diligence, and make sure you have a clearer understanding of what you are getting and what you are giving up.

After answering the diagnostic questions and visiting at least three solo practitioners, you might want to consider a hybrid solo practice. This would start with a very candid conversation with your senior partner. I do not recommend that you speak to anyone other than the person who would ultimately make the decision, as it can be seen as a mutinous act. Be prepared, however, because should the partner not be receptive, you might lose your job on the spot. Many lawyers, especially those entrusted with managing both small and large firms, are notoriously ego-driven and paranoid.

A sample conversation would begin: "Hello, Senior/Managing Partner. I would like to schedule a meeting with you to discuss ideas I have for the firm." Resist the "Let's talk now" or "Let's have a drink after work" or "Just give me a hint" response. This is not a conversation to have in the midst of his busy and hectic day, and it's not a barroom conversation. If he prods, say you have an idea on some productivity issues or something that will disinterest him.

Continue by asking, "When could we have a half hour to chat?" This will tell him that you do not have a five-minute question about the copy machine and that you think the issue is important enough to actually schedule a meeting. If he says two weeks, then wait. It will show him that it is important enough to wait but not so urgent that you are anxious for an answer.

Once the time for the meeting comes, shut the door, turn off your Blackberry, and speak face to face, being sure to make eye contact.

It helps to be prepared for the meeting with the following data:

1. Time you have worked at the practice;

2. Income or hours generated by your work; and

3. Current salary.

Open the conversation by saying, "Mr. Partner, I really enjoy working here; I respect you and the quality of work we produce. I would like to work here with you for the rest of my career if that is possible." Continue by reassuring him that you are not asking for a raise. This will disarm him since, I assure you, this is what he predicted was the basis of your meeting request.

"Could you please tell me your thoughts on my contribution to the firm?" While this may seem like you are fishing for a compliment or perhaps a raise—and that is partially true—you are setting the tone for the conversation to establish that you both have something at stake: for you, a job, income, and practice you enjoy; for him, a valued and trusted employee.

Once your value to the firm is established, tell him that you have been considering what it would be like to have your own law firm. (This is a thought that every lawyer who has ever employed another lawyer has considered, so he should not be surprised.)

"However, since we enjoy such a wonderful synergy, I would like to explore another option with you first, out of respect for you and the firm. In other words, I believe we can be more productive working together than apart." (If he does not agree to this, you might as well leave right then.)

"I yearn for more _____." (Insert the reason for wanting to start your law firm that you identified using the above diagnostic.) I will assume your reason is money, as that is usually the reason people give me for why they aspire to be solo practitioners. But since you told the partner that you were not looking for a raise, you must sandwich the issue of money between at least two other reasons.

Try something like this: "I am yearning for more trial experience, equity (code for money), and name recognition." Not bad, huh? What boss would not like to hear that? He'll think to himself, "This lawyer is ambitious, hardworking, and wants a stake in the outcome of the firm. How can we work to make this happen?"

If the boss gives the okay, then you may have all the benefits of your own law firm with none of the burden. You can continue to practice law, get clients, and not worry about changing the toilet paper in the bathroom.

Should he say no, or offer you something that is unacceptable, then you will spend the rest of your career showing him what a foolish mistake he made, and I will show you how. Keep reading.

3

Solo with Someone Else:
SHOULD YOU HAVE A PARTNER?

While in law school, you should be keenly aware that the students sitting around you will one day be your judges, senators, opposing counsel, referral sources, and partners.

If you are looking for a potential law partner, log on and register on www.makeityourownlawfirm.com for help finding someone who might be a good match. It is much less expensive to share the initial startup costs of a firm with another person rather than shoulder it all yourself. Imagine the cost of every copy machine, stapler, rent check, or computer. divided in two or three or five? Even better, you will have multiple fishing lines in the water—more cases and clients, and more income. Where you may be slow, hopefully your partners are not, and vice versa.

Picking the right law partners, however, is probably harder than finding the right life partner. *What?* Yes, it's true. You are not picking the partner because of love but because your synergy will create something stronger than you could create financially on your own. So what should you look for and how?

First, I suggest you look in the mirror and ask yourself the following:

1. What area of law will I practice?
2. What is my unique demographic?
3. What are my strengths?
4. What are my weaknesses?
5. What am I willing to do to make this partnership work?
6. What do I expect my partner to do?
7. What kind of financial commitment am I prepared to make to this?
8. What kind of time commitment am I prepared to make?
9. Where do I want to work?
10. What is my one-year, five-year, and ten-year plan?

If you have no business experience, look for someone who does. If you speak a foreign language, you could be an asset to someone who does not. Want to move elsewhere? Find someone with ties to that city.

Some practices go together like peanut butter and jelly. Criminal law and personal injury are a good mix because they often draw from the same client base, which can lead to cross referrals. And in a pinch, a criminal lawyer can cover a hearing for a personal injury lawyer, and vice versa. Volume immigration and traffic tickets form another good mix.

Some practices will be more like peanut butter and honey, not a classic but still pretty good. These combinations include, for example, family law and commercial litigation or estate planning and real estate.

However, some practices will not mix, especially when you consider having your clients sitting in the same waiting area as your partner's clients. Say you want to practice traffic ticket law, and your potential partner wants to do real estate closings for high-end residential buyers; that will not work. Your clients might call at all hours of the day, show up without appointments, or get belligerent in the reception area. Your partner's clients will expect to find a quiet conference room in which to review contracts. So, think about the potential client mix before forming a partnership with another lawyer. If you are not sure how things may play out, you have plenty of mentors and contacts to consult from the due diligence described in the previous chapters.

Work ethic is another important factor. I have seen lawyers work for me or rent space from me who are in the office all day, every day, like they are studying for a final in law school. I have seen others (usually those who have failed at flying solo) who never come in or who always come in late.

My career has had different phases, so I have experienced this phenomenon firsthand. I have, however, never had a partner. There were stages in my career when I worked all day, every day, from sunup until I could not see straight. There was a time, which I will refer to as my mid-career intermission and will detail later in this book in a section about staying healthy, when I did not come to the office for over a month. Of course, I checked my e-mail daily and spoke to the office a couple of times a week. I really did not work very hard, though, and I paid for it. However, this was a very rewarding experience in an unanticipated way.

I never had too much trouble getting up and coming to work. No one was there to dock my time or scold me for being late. Truth is, no one will be there for you, either, which is why I have seen some lawyers come in later and later every day.

Just think about that in terms of you and your potential partner. How would you feel if she regularly came in at 10:00 AM while you were at your desk every day at 7:00 AM? Or vice versa? If there is a prior clear understanding and agreement as to this, there should be no problem. Again, I think it pays to have someone who is not exactly like you and can perhaps work on a slightly different schedule. But you both need to be working and contributing on an even basis, or the partnership is destined to fail.

Another word about being partners: get it in writing. Get a partnership agreement, form a corporation, or get an accountant's input on what would work best for you and your partner. There are about as many variations of partnership agreements as there are stars in the heavens. I know it's not romantic and sounds a lot like a prenuptial, but partnerships fail for a variety of reasons—from death to being too successful.

Friends of mine, two young and very talented lawyers, had a nasty partnership breakup that cost them both a lot of energy and money. They say, "Hell hath no fury like a woman scorned," but that pales in comparison to the fury of a lawyer scorned.

You will find a sample partnership agreement as an appendix to this book. This should *not* be used or modified to set up your own partnership; I include it here only as a jumping-off point for thinking about issues to consider.

If you are reading this and are still in either college or law school, you should know that most schools will allow you to audit business and language courses for free. That means you can and should learn at least one other language (besides English) while you have the access to this resource. Think you are too busy now? I assure you, things get exponentially more difficult once you are out of school, so spend the time now to acquire this knowledge.

Out of school already? No problem. Go to your public library and read some books about business, marketing, and management. I cannot stand stale, textbook stuff, so I recommend reading things by people who have actually made or done something in their lives.

Here's a list of some of the books I have read that helped me a great deal in turning my law firm into a business.

- *Good to Great* by Jim Collins: This book was written by a university professor and his team. They did a very detailed analysis of why and how some good businesses become great and other good businesses fail.

- *The E-Myth* by Michael Gerber: This should be a mandatory read for anyone opening his or her own law firm. It has helped me identify the importance of working *on* my business instead of merely being trapped working *in* it.

- *Outliers* by Malcolm Gladwell. Gladwell is a writer for *The New Yorker* magazine. His books, *Blink: The Power of Thinking Without Thinking*, *The Tipping Point: How Little Things Make a Big Difference*, and *Outliers: The Story of Success*, are all excellent books to help you think in and out of the box about the choice you are making to go out on your own as well as the choices you will be faced with every day.

- *How to Start and Build a Law Practice* by Jay G. Foonberg. I read this book my third year out of law school, and my only regret is that I did not read it sooner. Mr. Foonberg has helped guide generations of lawyers to start and build their own law practices. I highly recommend it.

- *The Little Big Things: 163 Ways to Pursue Excellence* by Tom Peters. Peters is considered by many to be the guru of gurus in the world of crisis, leadership, networking, innovation, and design.

- *Think and Grow Rich* by Napoleon Hill. This is considered by many to be the single best book they have ever read. His devotees are cultlike in their belief in his methods and philosophies. This is another book I wish I had read in law school instead of after nearly twenty years of practice.

You are blessed with tremendous resources I did not have—including this book—so use them. The Internet did not exist when I started practicing law in 1991; with the click of your mouse, it will help you find resources that I did not know even existed.

Also, spend some money and time going to seminars on business.

Every lawyer I know goes to seminars on how to cross-examine an expert or how to comply with the latest statutes on lending law. We do this because we are conditioned by our experience in law school to think that possessing the most knowledge on the law is the only important skill a lawyer must possess. This is wrong in general and even more wrong for those who open their own law firms. Having your own law practice will demand that you are knowledgeable on the latest areas of negotiation, leadership, marketing, and management. To spend twenty hours a year in legal seminars and not know how to use Facebook or Twitter to build your practice is a costly mistake. To thrive on your own, you need to be an excellent marketer and manager as well as a great lawyer.

FINDING <u>YOUR</u> LAWYER AND ACCOUNTANT

You will need to retain a lawyer and an accountant, *especially* if you are a lawyer and an accountant yourself. I hate to repeat the old saying about the lawyer who represents himself having a fool for a client (but I just did, in case you had not heard it before or have not heard it in a while!). In other words, you need a lawyer. You need someone who can review your lease and partnership agreement and can serve as your registered agent so that should you get served, the process server does not come into your office and embarrass you in front of your staff or clients. You need a lawyer you can trust who will not bill you for every tiny little thing, but you need one who is not going to do you any favors, either.

Since I began practicing, I have had to hire many lawyers for a variety of reasons. They have defended me in lawsuits brought by disgruntled employees and suppliers, negotiated leases, and represented me on issues with the court and the bar. Hey, it's all part of being a lawyer. Stuff will happen—just do not represent yourself when it does.

How do you find a lawyer? Well, you have met a bunch by now and may have developed relationships with some whom you feel you can trust. If not, you are going to have to interview some to find out if you feel comfortable with them. I like sole practitioners. I think they understand my practice and the pressures involved better than the mega-law-firm type. It is not like you will have your lawyer on a retainer or will even need him or her more than a few times in your career, but at some point you *will* need a lawyer.

Here are some questions to consider asking your lawyer:

1. What experience do you have in small businesses or small law firms?

2. What will you charge?

3. Will I get you or an associate when I call?

4. Will I get you or an associate to do my work?

5. Will you review leases and contracts?

6. Do you litigate?

7. Have you ever been sued? Who did you use?

8. Can I call you on nights and weekends if I need to?

9. Who covers for you when you are sick or on vacation?

10. Have you ever had a bar grievance? How did you defend it?

Hey, if you cannot ask these questions and feel comfortable with the answers, you have the wrong lawyer. My business lawyer is a very smart and detailed guy who can do a real estate closing for me or set up a limited partnership. I trust him and like him.

You will need a C.P.A. as well. I have two. One, Manny Diaz who is truly a C.P.A., is on site several days per week and reconciles and balances my trust, operating, and personal accounts (more on this later), and the other makes sure that I pay every cent of tax I owe. I trust and like both very much, but I constantly find ways and debate ideas with them as to how my business can make more money and be more efficient.

When you start, you may not have too much cash flow to worry about. I am no accountant, but I can assure you they know more than you or me on how to maximize the benefits of owning your own law firm. Since you can easily give your accountant virtual access to your books or e-mail reports, the days of having someone on site may soon be over. Here are some questions to ask your accountant:

1. What experience do you have in counseling small business owners or law firm owners?
2. What do you charge?
3. How often will you check on me?
4. Will you have someone reconcile my accounts?
5. Will you advise me on payroll taxes, etc.?
6. Will you prepare all tax returns?
7. If I am audited, will you defend me?
8. Can I reach you after hours or on weekends if need be?

Knowing how to operate a business, get clients, and hire and fire staff are as important as understanding the latest immigration law update. Read this part carefully: *not more important, but as important.* Look, if you are not reading this book to learn how to own your own practice or make money, then close it now. If you want to read a book about how to be the best lawyer the world has ever known, pick up any book by Gerry Spence (the best lawyer the world has ever known) and read it. I am arguing that you need to know how to get clients and keep them, how to balance a trust account, and how to hire a secretary. Do not worry. I am going to tell you how in the next chapter; just keep reading.

4

Now What?
HOW, WHERE, AND WHEN DO I START?

Okay, we have made it this far. You have decided you do, in fact, want to be a lawyer. You have met with and spent time with lawyers who do and do not practice in the area in which you want to practice. You have decided you want a partner or want to open your own law firm.

Now what? Where do I start and when? You start now. If you wait until you have graduated, it will not be too late—just that much harder. Waiting to see if you get a job? I understand the motivation from having been in law school myself, but even if you get a job, it can be taken away before you even start or once you start or really at any minute with or without any notice. At least by opening your own law firm, you literally cannot be fired.

So, here is a checklist. Let's see what you have gotten done.

1. I have decided I truly, passionately want to be a lawyer.

   _____

2. I have decided what area of the law I want to focus on.

   _____

3. I have at least narrowed my focus to no more than three compatible areas. _____

4. I have met at least three lawyers who are considered the best in my state at what I want to do. _____

5. I have found a law partner. _____

6. I know what town I want to work and live in. _____

7. I have attended at least three social events with lawyers in my practice area of choice. _____

8. I joined the prevailing bar association for lawyers in my practice area of choice. _____

9. I have included in my studies foreign language and business classes. _____

10. I have a one-year, five-year, and ten-year idea of where I want to be. _____

11. I have consulted with both a lawyer and an accountant to help me select the best business entity for me._____

Okay, the plane is revved up, and there is gas in the tank. Where do we go? My advice is that you do not move off the runway until you have the previous ten things done. Moving forward without those things in line will only cost time and money down the road. Please note that these things are not in stone. You may be absolutely convinced from the brief amount of time you spent in divorce court that you want to be a family law lawyer, only to do it for a month and hate it. Things change. So will you.

5 Staff:
HIRING, FIRING, WHEN, WHERE, AND HOW

"Paging Mrs. Moneypenny. Mrs. Moneypenny, call on line two."

No employee will ever care more about you, your firm, your clients, or your future than you do. Do not ever forget that. Avoid years of disappointment and frustration and learn this lesson now. No matter how much you pay your staff or how much you love them or trust them, they will not and cannot care about you, your clients, your firm, or your future as much as you do. Sounds simple, right? It's not. Many of you reading this have never had an employee before. Many of you have never been an employee, either.

To me it was a bitter surprise—more true with secretaries than with other lawyers—to learn that they *did* care, just not as much as I did. They may care about getting your pleadings filed, but if they are late, it is your ass. They may care about you winning your trial, but you lose, and it's your responsibility. They may care that the office is clean, but go out of town, and the toilet paper may not get replaced for a week. This happened to me. I went out of town for a week to take depositions in Mississippi. I flew back and raced to the office, not even taking the time to go home and change. In the reception area, I stepped over menus with footprints on them. After washing my hands in the bathroom sink, I reached for paper towels. None. I looked for toilet paper. None. I looked in the cupboard for both. None.

At that time, I had a full-time office manager (no longer with the firm), two associates, one of whom was my first cousin (no longer with me), a receptionist (no longer on staff), and two secretaries (both gone).

I was shocked and angry and wet. Later, I asked the secretary, "Why are there no paper towels or toilet paper?"

She said, and I will never forget this, "We haven't had any for a week." I wanted to know what they were using instead but was too afraid and mad to ask. Bottom line: they care, but not ever as much as you will.

DO YOU NEED TO HAVE A SECRETARY TO BE A LAWYER?

I am surprised how many people ask me about hiring secretaries before they have even graduated law school. I guess it goes back to that delusional image many of us share: being a lawyer means having a hot secretary waiting for you at the door of your office with a cup of coffee in one hand, while you walk in and toss your hat on the hat rack. Get over this idea now.

Unless you have the business and money, secretaries can and will only cost you time and money. Plus, chances are you will hire the wrong person. Why? In the next paragraph is my theory on what you will have as staffing options. Keep in mind that this might be somewhat different in light of the current economic depression; however, the universal theme will be the same.

First, the best and brightest law students will generally be graduating from the best and brightest law schools. Those lucky few will generally go to the highest bidder, generally some big, fancy law firm named after partners who are long dead. Those country-club law firms usually hire the best and brightest secretaries. They can and will pay them more than you will probably be making in your first few years as a lawyer. They will give them insurance and parking and paid vacations. They will pay them overtime and order a cake for them each time they make it another year. They give out things like bonuses and cost of living wage increases. Those secretaries also supposedly possess the knowledge and skill to handle the most complex of legal tasks, justifying their salaries and those of the lawyers for whom they work. Most of them will have more years of legal experience than you have been alive. Forget them. You will never be able to afford them or keep them happy with your little law firm.

Then, as in a food chain, the skill level and professionalism slowly drop as you move down to the second- and third-tier firms. Assuming you are starting your own firm right out of law school, you are the equivalent of a movie that has not yet been rated and goes straight to video.

So, what's left? The rejects, burnouts, and those who do not know anything but are willing to learn. All of that is great except that unless your client asks you about Shelley's Rule or some such mindless stuff that only appears in a law school exam, you will not have much to teach. Yet.

So, now what do you do? Before I teach you how to hire an assistant, let me teach you how to fire one. Why? Because hiring is easy, and firing is sometimes almost impossible.

GOLDEN RULE 1: FIRE FAST AND HIRE SLOW.

Let's begin with firing, since firing an employee is one of the most difficult things I have had to do as the owner of my own law firm. I estimate that I have probably had several hundred employees in nearly twenty years of practice. Most have been fired, some have quit, others went to lunch and never came back, and some are still here.

It may have something to do with my own experiences in life, but rejecting someone or throwing them out has always been very tough for me. Also, I have made the regrettable mistake of befriending my employees. Let me make this clear: when I say *befriend*, I mean I considered them my best friends.

Bottom line: it is a business, and if the person is neither making you money nor making your life easier, fire them. You will be amazed how good you feel afterward and how much you regret that it took you so long.

When firing an employee, it makes sense to document everything. Think like a lawyer. If the employee is constantly late, has missed a deadline, lies, or does any number of other things that are unacceptable, put it in writing and give the list to him or her. When you notify the person that he or she is fired, make sure you have someone there with you, if at all possible. Get the fired employee out of the office immediately. If the person asks for notice and is willing to work, you should refuse the offer in all but the most unusual circumstances. This is also true for the employee who quits. Pay the employee his or her severance if you feel it is necessary or legally required, and escort the person out of the building yourself.

When I fire an employee, I rarely tell them the truth as to why they are being fired. I am sure if any of my former employees are reading this, they are probably cursing me once again. First of all, the truth is very hard for some people to hear, and it usually only escalates an already traumatic and potentially dramatic scene. I do not want to argue or be persuaded to reconsider. I just want them out. It sounds easy, but it has taken me nearly twenty years to learn.

You will probably hate me for sharing this with you, but I have gotten so good at firing staff quickly that this year I had to let someone go who had just returned from her honeymoon and another while she was out of town because of a death in the family.

You do not want to give the severance check on the spot. You want it to be mailed to the person in two weeks, when they would have earned it. You do this for two reasons: First, why advance money until it would have been due? Second, you want to make sure the person is somewhat helpful over the next couple of weeks, as you might have to contact them to ask questions about pending matters.

I have been amazed at how little I have missed people professionally once they have left the office. I am even referring to people who worked for me for five or six years; the office continued like they had never been there. Do not fall into the trap that has enslaved me for nearly twenty years. You do not need any single employee other than yourself to survive.

So, what about the exit survey for the employee who quits? Do you care? I do. I want to know why an employee quits. What did I do or not do that made leaving my office the better move for them? I guess it is imaginable that employees probably do not tell me the truth, either. Therefore, I am most likely destined to repeat the mistakes that I made, just like fired employees are most likely destined to repeat their own mistakes somewhere else.

A checklist for firing an employee is below:

1. Document the employee's unacceptable behavior.

2. Change passwords on computers.

3. Fire the employee with a witness present, if possible.

4. Obtain the employee's key to the office and his or her parking card.

5. Change voicemail pass codes.

6. Review all pending e-mails and have future e-mails redirected to you or to an assigned staff member.

7. Get a forwarding e-mail for them.

8. Get a forwarding phone and address for them.

9. Do not give the severance check on the spot; instead, tell them it will be mailed.

10. If employees quit, ask them how you can be a better boss in the future.

You may also wonder what to say when former employees are interviewing for new jobs and you are called as a reference. There are some laws on this, and you should check with the attorney you hired to help you set up your firm. Regardless, unless you know the other employer well, I suggest you do not go into much detail. Just say that you could not afford the person or that the project she was working on fizzled out. Do not badmouth them. After all, they need a job and may one day refer a case to you.

GOLDEN RULE 2: DO NOT SLEEP WITH YOUR STAFF.

I think that when you are thrown into a very intense situation like a solo practice and you spend eight to twelve hours a day with the same people—laugh with them, cry with them, eat meals with them, party with them, roll their wheelchair-bound fathers down wedding aisles, share secrets and dreams with them—instances of intimacy are bound to happen. It is, after all, a very lonely way to make a living.

Imagine you are in a deposition for eight hours in Mississippi. When it is over, your assistant calls to see how it went. You are tired. You are scared about the testimony and your chances of winning the case. She listens. She understands. You call your wife, and she does not even ask about it—or maybe she doesn't even answer the phone. Before you know it, you start sharing more of how you feel about this case, that case, this employee, that idea with your assistant. "Let's have lunch and talk about the case," you say. "Let's have drinks after work and decompress."

I have never slept with any of my employees, but I sure have been close. And it will be very tempting for you, married or not, when faced with an offer by an attractive assistant to have sex. I am not a labor lawyer, but I am sure it would be suicidal to ever suggest that any of you reading this even consider it. But, beyond the legal ramifications, in all but the most unusual circumstances, it will hurt your practice and your life.

I will tell you that I have had very unprofessional friendships with both the men and women I have worked with. Part of it is my personality, for sure. I like to hug and kiss people. I like to joke around and be myself. I tell people that I love them when I do. I cross and push the limits and boundaries all the time. I am not a lecherous pervert, but I am who I am, and I think I would hate working in an office where I could not be myself.

GOLDEN RULE 3: DO NOT BECOME BEST FRIENDS WITH YOUR STAFF.

So, what's the problem with being buddy-buddy with your employees? Won't they work harder for you since you are their best friend, too? Absolutely not. As long as you are paying them and they report to you, then nothing you can do or say to me will convince me that you are best friends with any of them. What about Oprah and Gayle? Well, I do not know the intricacies of their relationship, but I suspect that while they may say they are best friends and may even believe that they are, as long as Gayle depends on Oprah for a paycheck or even a part of one, they are not.

Let me share with you something from my own personal experience. I have had a couple of people work for me who I thought were my best friends, whatever that means. They would listen to me, yes. I paid them for that. They told me their personal stuff, I guess, but I was paying them for that, too. They cared about my well-being, I guess, but I was their boss. They made me laugh, invited me to their weddings, rubbed my shoulders, brought me cookies, came to my kids' parties, answered my calls on the weekends ... stop me when you hear anything that sounds like anything more than an employee trying to keep his or her job. Bottom line: hire employees to do their jobs, not to be your buddies.

Ever try to fire someone you thought was your best friend? Good luck. By now, they know your insecurities, your trigger points, and your secrets. I tried to fire one woman for five years. I never could because almost every time I finally got the courage up to let her go, she did something that made me believe I could not practice law without her. She would get a case resolved. She would find a missing file or point out an issue I had overlooked. She had me whipped. She was not very good most of the time, but she was amazingly good once in a while. I was confused. She knew me, my practice, and my clients, but she just was not giving me her all. She gave me just enough to keep her working for me for almost six years. Finally, tormented, I let her go. She now works for one of the largest personal injury law firms in the country and still remains a friend—just not my best friend.

GOLDEN RULE 4: HIRE SOMEONE WHO CAN DO WHAT YOU CANNOT.

You have to hire someone who knows what you do not. That means an experienced secretary with access to forms and practical know-how. You can and should find out if any of the secretaries you met at the lawyers' offices (*See why I had you get their names and numbers?*) knows anyone who would be willing to work after hours, on the weekends, or part-time to help you. They all know someone.

You can also put an ad on Craigslist (which draws a younger and less sophisticated demographic), Monster.com, and Career Builder. Consider posting on the website of your local law school or a paralegal or legal administrator's career placement Internet bulletin board. When looking for legal assistants, I have hired a number of lawyers who do not really want to practice law or cannot handle the stress and would rather have a simple nine-to-five job. Your ad needs to be as specific as possible, detailing exactly what you are looking for. So, before you write an ad, let's figure what you need.

First, in Miami, where I live and practice, I need an assistant who can speak both English and Spanish. Nearly all of my clients speak and write Spanish; most do not know any English. That will automatically eliminate seventy percent of potential candidates.

Second, I need a secretary who knows Microsoft Word and Office. Sounds basic, right? Wrong. Many people applying for the job may have little to no computer knowledge. Times are changing, but older people may have grown up in the dictation and handwritten calendar age.

Third, I need someone who does not smoke. This may sound like I'm looking for a lawsuit, but it's for several reasons. (This will undoubtedly disturb some of you who are smokers. Candidly, I hope that it does enough to make you reconsider your dangerous and time-wasting habit.) Smokers, I have found, need to take smoking breaks when they are stressed. Working for me is very stressful. I do not want to call the office and find out that my assistant is smoking in the parking lot. Nor do I want us to be in court and have her run out to take a puff break. I am also very allergic to it. It drives me nuts. Sounds insane until you have a secretary whom you cannot stand to be around because you simply cannot breathe. It has happened.

Fourth, she needs to be able to multitask. Why? Because I am a multitasker. I will give her several things to do and then interrupt her with something else. Some can handle this; some cannot, and they do not last for very long with me.

Fifth, I have to like the person. He does not have to be my best friend. In fact, I prefer that he is not. More about that stupid mistake has already been mentioned, but I generally have to like the person. I am proud to say that right now, for probably the first time in my entire career, I very much like everyone who works for me. Hallelujah!

You may think that you would never hire someone that you do not like, and you are probably right. However, the person you hire is often not the same person who shows up to work at your office, and firing them is an entirely different animal. So, before you start interviewing any potential staff members, answer the following five questions:

1. My assistant must possess the following skills:

    _____

    _____.

    (Be as descriptive as possible.)

2. My assistant needs to have the following personality traits:

    _____

    _____.

    (Again, this is between you and me, so be as honest as possible.)

3. My assistant needs to work these hours:

    _____.

4. My assistant needs to work these days:

    _____.

5. My assistant needs to have this much experience: _____. (Careful with this one! Someone can have twenty years of experience and not know as much as you think someone with one year of experience would have. So, instead of putting a year amount, (for example, five years), be specific. Identify skills like setting mediations, filing pleadings, preparing real estate closings, and writing wills. Whatever you need, put that down.)

6. My assistant needs _____ references. (Indicate a number.)

7. My assistant needs to be able to travel for work: yes_____ no_____ (Check one.)

8. My assistant needs to be able to go to hospitals, clients' houses, and court: yes_____ no_____ (Check one.)

Once you've reviewed the list, it's time to take a look in the mirror. Who are you, and what does your office look like? If you have a busy, fast-paced, and chaotic office, admit that. If you have one of those phone-never-rings, you-can-hear-a-pin-drop offices, admit that. If you are hard-driving or low-key, be honest—admit it.

I often describe my office as akin to the triage area of a metropolitan emergency room. Phones are ringing. Clients show up. Lawyers are scrambling. It is fast-paced, chaotic, and exciting.

Are you an organized control freak or a total mess? Or something in between? Are you on time or always late? Are you a workaholic, or do you hardly work? You need to be honest so that the ad you create helps eliminate those who may not be the right fit for you right off the bat.

I am, probably not to your surprise, a disorganized mess. I rarely know what day or time it is. I am totally focused on the task at hand and forget to eat or that I have a meeting in a half hour. I am almost always late. I procrastinate and lose focus. I get bored and on and on. (I told you I would be honest!)

Where is your office? Big building, no parking, downtown, the Everglades? You need to know. My office is in the middle of Coral Gables, which is generally considered to be a very desirable place to work. That has helped me find better people.

What kind of law do you practice? If it is wills and estates, you can say that, but you will get a wills and estates person. If it's divorce, well, you will get a divorce law assistant. And maybe that is all some lawyers need or want. Not me, though, and not you. You want someone who at least will look at this as more than a job. Even if it is just slightly more, it will be more than nothing.

The kind of people I have found to be the best employees are usually those who need the job. Spoiled little girls and boys who show up in nicer cars than mine have rarely, if ever, worked out. Single mothers, college students, homeowners, and my all-time favorite, former military officers, have made the best employees. People who have pride in their appearance and work will be the best.

Here is a typical ad that I would post:

> Busy and exciting [describe it accurately but in the best light] Coral Gables trial law firm [we are not a settlement mill, and location is important] needs an energetic, organized, and disciplined person [suggest that this is not going to be an easy job and that there will be accountability] who is passionate about helping injured people [code for plaintiff's personal injury] rebuild their lives. Must know Microsoft Word, Outlook, and Spanish. Must have experience in

drafting pleadings, jury instructions, set for hearings, etc. Salary and benefits are commensurate with experience. [Why bind yourself to anything?]

E-mail resume, a writing sample, and at least three recommendations to: lawyer@makingityourownlawfirm.com

Why an e-mail? Do you really want to tie up your fax machine and phone all day? E-mails also will allow you, if the applicants are unsophisticated, to look at the metadata embedded in their cover letters, résumés, and writing samples. More than once, we have uncovered forged documents.

I am not just pretty bad at hiring people—I am horrible. So, I usually get out of the way and delegate the task of screening to someone else. As a solo practitioner, however, you will have to spend the time and money to sift through each applicant yourself.

Think a headhunter or temp agency is any better? Think again. They only get paid if they place the person—sometimes exorbitant amounts. They are going to hide blemishes and distort the truth more than those who are submitting the references. Run the other way.

Isolate the top five candidates and have someone you trust meet them first. Just like what happened to me when I was looking for a job as a lawyer, be careful that an insecure assistant trying to protect her own job security does not block a truly talented candidate.

Have a list of questions prepared for the person in advance. Then shut up and listen. If you have done most of the talking in the interview, as in Voir Dire, then you have not learned enough about the person you are interviewing.

Below are some questions I like to ask:

1. **You walk into the office. The lights are off. There is a client waiting who has no appointment but has brought a friend who needs a lawyer. There is a dirty menu on the floor. Your phone is ringing: the lawyer is calling you from the**

road because he forgot the address of the courthouse. You have not put on your makeup yet. You have to clock in. You have perishable items in your lunch bag that need to be refrigerated. What do you do first?

There may not be any wrong or right answer, but if telling me where the courthouse is located is not in the top two, she is going to be the wrong hire.

2. **What did you like most about your last job?**

If she says, "Everything," you had better find out why she left from someone other than her.

3. **What did you like least about the job?**

If she says, "Nothing," she is not telling you the truth. Use the word *job* instead of asking about her boss. Many applicants, however, have told me scathing things about their former employers. I can only imagine what mine must say about me.

4. **Where do you want to be in five years?**

If she says, "Working for you," she's certainly clever and well rehearsed.

5. **Five years ago, where did you think you would be today?**

Whatever she says, compare it to where she actually is and what she has been doing. In all fairness, if you asked me fresh out of high school where I wanted to be in five years, I would not have said, "In a law school library, studying civil procedure." So, be generous with younger applicants.

6. **What questions do you have for us?**

If her first question involves holidays off, overtime, personal days, raises, or bonuses, you have got someone who has only one concern: herself. Look for the first question to be about your cases, clients, or aspirations; and beware if they have *no* questions.

GOLDEN RULE 5: DO NOT HIRE ANYONE WHO CANNOT KEEP A JOB FOR MORE THAN A YEAR OR TWO.

If you see a resume for an applicant who has had ten jobs in three years (and those are just the ones she is actually revealing), run the other way. Also, be afraid of somebody who is about to graduate from school and studying in an area completely different from law.

GOLDEN RULE 6: DO NOT BUY WITHOUT A TEST DRIVE.

A lot of applicants will say they can do things. No problem. Do not wait until you hire them to find out. If you need an assistant to type letters, set hearings, calendar lunches, or whatever, ask her to do those things right then and there. If the applicant hems or haws or says she is nervous, take a pass. Really, how hard is it to schedule a lunch with your friend? If the applicant says she knows how to screen potential bankruptcy clients, go into another room and pretend to call her and see how she responds to your typical bankruptcy client's first call.

GOLDEN RULE 7: DO NOT HIRE ON THE SPOT.

Do not—no matter how desperate you are or how great the candidate looks—hire him or her on the spot. Always ask for a second interview. You would be surprised to find out how many times I have loved a candidate only to have her not show up for the second interview or come as almost an entirely different person than the one I met or thought I met on the first go-around.

GOLDEN RULE 8: ALWAYS CALL THEIR FORMER EMPLOYERS.

It is not enough just to call the employers who are on the reference list. The reference is not always the person to whom they reported. I have had a number of fired staff immediately get new jobs. When I see their current employers and they tell me this person or that person is now working for them, I ask why they never called me to get my opinion. Some, I guess, did not care; others said they had called and spoken to someone who claimed to have been the person's supervisor and gave a great recommendation. I suspect that one assistant will help another— two bad apples in the same bushel.

GOLDEN RULE 9: PERFORM BACKGROUND CHECKS.

Have a private investigator perform background checks, using both current and any former or maiden names. Use one of the many Internet sites available for doing background searches. I have hired convicted felons, sex addicts, transsexuals, strippers, recovered drug addicts, disbarred lawyers, and doctors because they told me the truth and I believe in giving people second chances. I have also *almost* hired a number of the above but did not when they lied to me about their pasts in their interviews. You should never hire a liar.

GOLDEN RULE 10: BE UP FRONT ABOUT HIRING AWAY FROM FIRMS.

If you hire someone away from another firm, be up front about it. Tell the other firm. Get their permission if there is a conflict, or just let them know if there is not.

I once hired a secretary from a law firm that I had a very substantial case against. My office administrator (no longer with me) was told to make sure that the other firm did not object to the hiring. She was told by the new secretary (no longer with me) that they did not object and that a letter confirming that was forthcoming. The letter never came.

I lost the secretary, the office manager, and the case over a conflict of interest. The worst part was I never received any information from this secretary, and I think she never really had any.

I was devastated by this. It reminded me just how lonely a solo practice can be. I remember returning to the office after the judge conflicted me out of the case and staring at the twenty employees I had, including three associates, and shaking my head with disbelief at how careless my staff was with my clients, my firm, and my life.

Another firm recently took one of my most beloved staff members away by, I assume, offering her more money and less responsibility. The other lawyer was a former classmate of mine whom I had a number of cases with in the past, but none pending. He did not call me right away but did several weeks later. I was both pissed off and hurt. I took it horribly that I had lost the assistant whom I cared for so much. I felt abandoned and betrayed by her since she had never told me that she was in any way unhappy with our working relationship. Until that moment, I would have trusted her with my life. Welcome to having your own law firm.

GOLDEN RULE 11: YOU DO NOT ALWAYS—IF EVER—GET WHAT YOU PAY FOR.

I have had incredible team members whom I have paid very little for, and I have had horrible ones who demanded outrageous salaries and produced nothing. I had one who asked for nearly the same salary as me. He agreed to take a significant cut in his salary for a short period of time to prove his worth to me. Not only did he fail to prove his worth, he made matters worse by making mistakes that cost the firm time and money. Ask around and find out what people make in your community. Check out the United States Department of Labor's Bureau of Labor Statistics site for some additional clues: http://www.bls.gov/oes/2009/may/oes232011.htm.

A word about bonuses and raises: Times have certainly changed recently, and most employed people are just glad they have jobs. So am I. But when times were different, I was faced with the challenge of when and what to give as bonuses and raises. You can never be right. No matter how much you give and when you give it, it is never enough. If you expect some big pat on the back because you give an extra couple thousand dollars at Christmastime, do not hold your breath.

I have always believed that bonuses and raises should be based upon the profit of the firm and the value of the employee's contribution. The problem is that many, if not most, of the people I have employed have not felt that way. I have had many stressful arguments in trying to get my staff to be more entrepreneurial and rewarded by performance. I have given up, since most people, with few exceptions, who work as support staff in law firms are not entrepreneurial by nature. I accept that now and will not spend energy trying to convert them.

One year, I naively concocted a bonus plan that rewarded the team on the number of cases we resolved. In Florida, you cannot split fees with non-lawyers, so this was done on a quantity basis without regard to dollar value. For every case that we settled, X dollars were put in a kitty that was to be split at the end of the year. This plan was so flawed from the beginning that I am embarrassed to admit to you that I even did it. The good news was that we did, in fact, settle a lot of cases—more than I had in many years. The bad news was that while the cases were settled, they were often not closed out, as all of the firm's energy was focused on settling the next cases. So, we started to have a backlog of settled but unclosed files. In addition, a rift developed in the office because most members of the staff were far less productive than one employee. In other words, her star started to rise because of her performance, which created a rift in the fragile team dynamic. It was like the television show *Survivor*, with factions and side deals. Before the end of the year, two of the staff members were fired, the third was on maternity leave, and my superstar left to find another universe to illuminate. I was now alone except for just one employee. The cases kept getting settled.

The other fatal flaw of that plan was that the value of cases settled had no relationship to the profit of my firm. Who cares if you settle thirty cases or three hundred if you are not making any money? Bottom line: bonuses have to be related to firm profits.

GOLDEN RULE 12: DON'T TELL YOUR STAFF YOU'RE BROKE WHILE SPENDING THE SUMMER IN ITALY.

Your staff rarely, if ever, will understand or even care if your firm is making money or not. They may see the occasional "big settlement" and believe it all goes into your pocket. Most do not know or care about the overhead, insurance, salaries, taxes, or anything other than what they get to take home each week. Very few of my staff ever owned their own businesses, much less law practices, before they worked for me.

So, when they see you drive a fancy car or travel to far-off places, it is natural that they think you can afford to pay bonuses or raises—whether or not you can or should. Just keep that in mind. If you tell someone no bonuses and then go buy yourself a Rolex, you're in for some resentment.

On the other hand, if you have an excellent employee who is loyal and honest and productive, pay that person as much as you can to keep them. For some reason, my best employees have never really been about the money. One in particular was my beloved receptionist. I joked for the years she was there that she was doing the work of five people and only getting paid for two. It was not so funny when she left. I offered to double her salary, but she could not be persuaded to stay. I offered to change her job role, responsibilities, and hours—anything she wanted. But, no—she wanted to go.

When she left, I found out that I had been really wrong: she was doing the job of six people, and even six people could not do the job as well as she had. We stayed in touch, mostly because she was and is the rare employee/friend who was truly my friend after all.

For the years that followed, I lamented to her how much my office and I really missed her. Finally, nearly three years later, she came back.

I hope that, if you and I meet at an event after this book is published, she will have organized it and will be there so that I can introduce you to this very special person.

A FEW LAST THOUGHTS ON STAFFING

Spend some time researching the latest phenomenon: the virtual assistant. I have not yet experienced this personally (maybe by the time I publish this book I will have), but I have spoken to a number of lawyers who have had very good experiences with virtual assistants. A virtual assistant is a person (possibly in another city, state, or country) who works for you as though they are working in your office. The advantages are astounding: lower compensation, less required office space, employee prescreening, availability in other time zones (they work while you sleep), and higher education. I read an entire book on the subject, entitled, *The Four-Hour Work Week* by Timothy Ferriss, and I recommend it.

You are going to have to learn a lot on the fly by asking questions. While my mentor team was very helpful to me, so were, in large part, their secretaries. A Nordstrom gift certificate or an envelope with a few hundred dollars in it goes a long way to making sure that a secretary will answer your questions the next time you need to know how to subpoena a non-party witness or file a lien.

It is also essential that you hire someone you can absolutely trust; it may take years to find this person. You need to know how to do everything yourself. That means you need to know how to draft pleadings, schedule hearings, or record liens—whatever is appropriate for your area of practice. You have to learn how to do all of this. It means getting out there, asking questions, and probably making a few mistakes along the way.

I also recommend that you should not represent a client unless you are really familiar with the ins and outs of how to handle their case. Instead, you should co-op or co-counsel the case with one of your mentors. Some mentors who are true friends will do it for free. I have been blessed with such a man—Ken Bush. Others will want a percentage of the fee.

There will come a time when you will need some office help who do not need to be like Mrs. Moneypenny. When you find yourself spending too much time and energy on clerical stuff like photocopying, filing, and mailing, you need to get help. You can probably find a high school, college, or law student who would be happy to spend time in your office for a minimal salary so they too can start the due diligence of being a lawyer that you did in the earlier chapters.

What about the phones? My practice lends itself to having a live person answering the phones. I have not made the leap to having that done outside of the office, which is in part due to the call volume. Some practices, however, with large call volumes and an IP line can have their phones answered by an answering service. I do not like answering services myself, so I have never used one. It always seems obvious that the person answering is not in the lawyer's office.

Also, you will be blessed with the use of technologies I did not have when I was starting out that will allow you to, for example, dictate letters that are transcribed by voice recognition software or outsource word processing to virtual assistants.

6 THE OFFICE

OFFICE SPACE

I have seen many solo practitioners spend massive fortunes on their offices—maybe to impress themselves, their friends, or the imaginary clients and secretaries they think they will soon have. Mostly, I think it's still part of that delusional and outdated concept of what they think being a lawyer is all about.

I started my practice in the same apartment I had in law school, and I would probably still be there if not for some great advice from a brilliant accountant, Jon Stoller, who was himself once a lawyer. I remember our phone call very clearly. I was calling him from my kitchen, where I was standing naked, eating ice cream. I told him that I had decided to start my own law firm.

"Great," he said. "Where is your office?"

"Why do I need an office?" I asked. "Why spend the money? I can meet clients at Wendy's, their homes, or their offices. If I need a conference room, I can use the one at the law school library." And for about three months I did.

He said something that changed my career. He told me that I had to get up, get dressed, and go to an office. I had to look and feel like a lawyer to be a real lawyer. I guess that real lawyers do not practice law naked in their law school apartments.

So I started to look for office space. At first I went to places I thought I wanted to be. I looked at South Beach. I liked South Beach, and I figured it would be a good place to spend my days. Thankfully, it was too expensive, and office space on Ocean Drive at that time was virtually nonexistent.

I then looked at downtown. I went to the fanciest building and looked at a space that a lawyer was subletting. He wanted one thousand dollars a month, not including parking. Downtown traffic was thick and confusing; parking was nearly impossible.

I was in his office suite, in what I learned was probably the most undesirable space, just about ready to commit to a lease, even though I felt no comfort in it. The sun shifted, and the late-afternoon Miami sun came beating through the window; I felt very uncomfortable. The room went from cold to blindingly hot. I shut the blinds, but the sun penetrated them. It was like I was in a sauna or some kind of torture chamber. I told the lawyer I could not take it—not at any price.

He tried to lure me in by suggesting that he could give me work to "help me get started." I had never thought of that before, but I have recommended it to many aspiring solo practitioners who are short on startup and long on time: offer to share space or sublet space from an existing law firm or lawyer in exchange for work. This kind of deal has to be very clear from the onset, and I suggest that it be in writing, not so much so that you have a contract, but rather to eliminate any confusion. Here are some things you need to know and have an agreement upon in such a deal:

1. How much space will you get? Will you have use of the common areas such as the conference room, kitchen, and reception area, or will you just have that blistering office at the end of the suite?

2. Will your contribution be in terms of time or dollars or both?

3. How much time will the lawyer want for the space?

4. Will you be able to use his staff for his stuff? Will he be able to use your staff for his stuff?

5. What if there is a conflict, for example, you have an 8:00 AM hearing and so does he?

6. There may be tax implications for you. Discuss this with your CPA.

7. Can you refuse particular assignments, or is it a no-choice deal?

8. How and when can you revise the deal if you find it does not turn out to be in your best interest?

9. Can you put your cards in the reception area?

10. Can you hire staff, and is there room for them?

11. Can your clients come in?

12. Can you use the office after hours?

13. Can you hang whatever you want on your walls?

14. Can you make popcorn if you like?

Being in a building with other lawyers is very important. The night after I turned down the lease, I went back to my apartment, feeling lost and a little dejected because I found myself again in my lonely apartment. It is one thing to live all alone, and it is another thing to live and work all alone, in all the same place.

The University of Miami is in Coral Gables. I had lived in Coral Gables for the past seven years, and it was the part of town I knew best and was most comfortable in. Most of the lawyers in Coral Gables at that time were solo practitioners. Most big firms were downtown, which has changed a little since I started.

So I started in Coral Gables because that is where I was most comfortable, and it was close, almost walking distance, to my apartment. You know, as a solo practitioner, you are not going to be making money sitting in traffic or on a bus. You need to be working and not just sitting.

My second piece of advice is that you should be somewhere you want to be. If you put your office, like your gym, in a place that is a hassle to get to, if you are at all like me, you will find more and more excuses why you cannot go there.

There is an argument for having no office at all—the virtual office. With laptops and Blackberries, do you really need to have a physical office? For the few who can get up each day and get out without having a specific place to go, I guess that would be okay. However, for most, and in particular those who are just starting out, I say no. Get yourself a real office.

So where should you go? Here are key factors to consider in selecting your office location:

1. Where do you like spending your time?
2. Where are you comfortable?
3. How far is the location from where you live?
4. If you do not live near your desired office, can you move closer and still be comfortable?
5. Is it safe?
6. What does it say about you as a lawyer? Remember, as my father often told me, I am not a nightclub or an Italian restaurant—I am a lawyer.
7. Is it client friendly or an impenetrable fortress surrounded by a maze?
8. Are there other lawyers in that area for referrals (which go both ways), companionship, and coverage?
9. Are you going to be stuck in a windowless box with no access to the public?

10. Are there a bank, FedEx box, post office, and courthouse within a reasonable distance?

11. Will you be able to attract staff to work with you there?

12. Where do your clients expect a lawyer like you to be?

13. What will your office address say about you?

I have tried hard my whole career not to be just another lawyer. I cannot stand the thought of being on a dimly lit floor of lawyers or having my name listed in the directory of a building where I am just one lawyer of many. Everything I have done, I have tried to do just a little differently—from my business cards to my logo.

Perhaps I would have been a different lawyer if I had opened my shop or hung my shingle, as Mr. Tralins suggested, on South Beach. Or perhaps the traffic-choked drive and distractions of South Beach would have destroyed me.

I have often told aspiring lawyers to go where their clients are. Make it easy for them to find you. Make your office a place where they will be happy and proud to refer their friends. Many of my clients have never been to a downtown office tower. I had never been to one either before I became a lawyer.

My office is in a free-standing building with plenty of parking. It was an art gallery before I took it over thirteen years ago. My name is on the side of the building as a constant reminder to all those who pass by my location. The building serves as a three-dimensional billboard. It is expensive—perhaps too expensive for a solo practitioner—but I shudder to think what my practice would look like if I were in some other place.

It also makes me feel good to go there. This is so important that it almost invaluable. The colors, the sound, the smell, and the type of coffee we serve are all, for better or worse, selected by me or by people I have hired who have more sense of style than I.

I like to think of my office as part of the experience of being my client, but you do not have to have your own building to have your own client experience. Just look for a space. Now more than ever, there is plenty of it. Choose something that is perhaps slightly off the beaten path, or maybe in a hotel, an upscale mall, or on the street. Make it yours so it reflects who you are and what message you want to send to your target client base. Choosing the wrong office could cost you more than you will ever know.

Many lawyers will gladly allow you to have your mail delivered to their offices and to use their conference rooms in exchange for a small fee. You can do this while you are physically in another office. It can become burdensome to have to pick up mail daily, though a courier could bring it to you, or to drive to that office only to find that a client doesn't show for his appointment. But it's an option, and it will give the impression to all but the cleverest observer that you, in fact, have your office there.

Since, in your due diligence efforts, you visited many lawyers and their offices and took copious notes, you can always emulate the things you liked. Early on in my career, I visited Gerry Spence's office. I saw framed verdicts and newspaper articles on the walls. I saw courtroom drawings of him in trial. I saw his ground-floor office and the wooden window blinds. I liked his style. I copied it and then added my own style.

Every couple of years, I move my desk around, repaint the walls, or buy a new chair. You should keep your office fresh and comfortable for you.

You should keep it clean. Maybe clients will notice the burned-out light bulb or the fingerprints on the glass of your conference room table. Maybe not. I am often accused of being obsessive about the light bulbs not being burned out in my office—it has driven some of my staff to quit, and others have been fired—but a burned-out light bulb says to me, "This lawyer is not a detail-oriented person, and I do not want him as my lawyer." I don't want my clients or opposing counsel ever saying or thinking that about me.

This stems, I am sure, from my childhood experiences of following my father around the video arcade game rooms that he owned and ran. I saw him literally make grown men cry if he found burned-out light bulbs. But it's more than that. You have to have and show pride in what you do and where you work.

Leasing office space now is like shooting fish in a barrel. You have a lot of choices and leverage. Demand a short-term lease with free or greatly diminished rent payments for the first six months or year. The payments can escalate as you get more established. Argue for free parking, signage rights, extra parking validations—anything. Shop around, and make sure you have the option to renew. If possible, rent just a little more space than you think you need. You will grow. It's easier to grow if you have the space. Get it before you need it, often at a premium price.

You will need at least four walls and a door for yourself. You will also need a place for clients to sit while they wait to be seen and someplace inviting for clients to meet with you. This can be in your office, but it would be better for the actual meeting to take place in a conference room so your office does not always have to be pristine. Further, you may have sensitive documents and other items in your office that you do not want to worry about accidently being seen by the wrong set of eyes.

You will need someplace to put a color copier, fax machine, and scanner. This can sit on your desk, and you can outsource any real document reproduction to a place like Sir Speedy or Kinko's. I will not give advice on anything I do not know; I stopped making copies myself long ago, but make sure you do some research on the latest technology in copiers and scanners.

We are moving our firm toward being paperless. With today's high-speed scanners and the enormous storage capacity of servers, being paperless is now a more realistic goal. I also have a small warehouse full of old files and exhibits that I spend money to store that could and should be scanned and destroyed. Had I started this process in the beginning, finding old files would be so much easier.

If you are not familiar with modern document technology, learn. Your old mentoring group may not be on the cutting edge of technology, so they may not be able to help you with this. (I have found that some very successful lawyers still calendar things in books and do not even have e-mail.) Read computer magazines, and take a class or hire someone to teach you how to use Microsoft Outlook, Windows, etc.

You need to research technology and see what is out there. I have already seen the changes in my time. I started when lawyers used black-and-white monitors and there was no Microsoft Windows. Data was stored on 5¼" floppy disks, and word processing involved a complex exercise in hitting the spacebar and shift keys in series. I was constantly losing everything I had written. Networks had not been invented yet. I could not send anyone a document unless I faxed it to them, and then they would have to retype the whole thing.

Invest some time and energy into finding an excellent computer geek or, what they like to be called, IT or Information Technology consultant. The IT guy you hire must be someone you can literally trust your life with, because, unless you are a computer genius, you will need to rely upon him to keep your office's computers/server running and to preserve and protect your data and recreate it if catastrophe should strike. Here are some questions to ask your IT guy:

1. Give me five references for solo practices or small firms you do work for.

2. What are your rates for nights, days, and weekends?

3. Who covers for you when you are sick or on vacation?

4. What is your disaster recovery plan for me?

5. What is your security plan for me?

6. What hardware do you recommend I use?

7. What payment arrangements can we make?

8. What if I am late with a payment? Do you charge interest?

9. What is your response time if I call you?

10. What is your preventative maintenance plan for me?

My IT guy, Urs Ebner, is Swiss. He is moody and a prima donna, and he is very expensive. I tried once to replace him with a cheaper company, and my computers immediately stopped working almost like clockwork. The modern law firm cannot function without its computers. Suddenly, we did not have our calendars, our clients' contact information, or even Google. You could hear the crickets chirp as my staff sat there paralyzed for days.

I had to go on my hands and knees and beg Urs to take me back as his client. Now his bills come in every month, I pay them, and my computers work. Another thing about computers I have learned the hard way is to replace them *before* they go down. Once they go down, the time and effort to replace them is exponential—and good luck recovering lost data! Find a reliable and dependable IT person who can and will be there for you night and day, and love him like he is your best friend.

You need a banker too. The value of having a working relationship with your banker is immeasurable. Find out which bank in town (I prefer small banks) likes to work with small businesses, especially law firms. Check with your mentors to find out which banks they recommend and why.

Go and meet the banker and explain that you are about to open your own law firm. You will need to have an operating account, a trust account (get the local rules from your state bar's website), a personal account, a business credit card, and perhaps a credit card processing machine. Some banks will extend small lines of credit to new lawyers, as we are generally considered a lower risk than most startup businesses.

Make sure your bank has online checking that will allow you to make transfers online between your accounts. Many banks today have special scanners at their ATMs that you can use to make deposits, which eliminates the need to spend time in line waiting for a teller.

It's also nice to have a bank that will work with your clients too. Some big, fancy banks will not accept clients that have only minimal balances.

Lines of credit are the lifeblood of my law practice. Income fluctuates, but hard overhead does not, so I often need help to make ends meet. You need to see what your bank is willing to do to help you. Most will require that you complete a financial statement. Your accountant can help you fill it out. You can find forms online and fill them out with Microsoft Word or QuickBooks.

Here are a few questions you need to ask your banker:

1. What will you charge me to open a business account?
2. Is there a minimum balance?
3. Does your bank work with lawyers on their trust accounts? Are you familiar with the bar rules?
4. Is there a particular person I can call when I need something?
5. Can you open accounts for clients I refer to you?
6. Can you give me a line of credit? If so, what are the rates?

GOLDEN RULE: GET A SCHEDULE AND SCHEDULE TIME TO GET CLIENTS.

In your calendar, you have to make sure you do not leave a day blank. Even if you are taking a day off (I recommend taking at least one day off each weekend), put that in your schedule. Here is a sample day in your calendar:

Monday

7:00 AM   Wake up

8:00 AM   Breakfast or coffee somewhere

9:00 AM	In the office; check e-mails and phone messages
10:00 AM	Read local, national, and legal papers and find legal and community events
12:00 AM	Lunch out of the office
1:30 PM	Call or send a note to one mentor to touch base
2:00 PM	Attend an event or volunteer at a charity
4:00 PM	Exercise at the gym
6:00 PM	Shop or have personal time and then go home

Consider this a typical day. You may say, "Well, great, Spencer. I did not accomplish a damn thing or make any money. What kind of B.S. book did you get me to buy?" That's partly true; you did not make any money that day. Welcome to the solo law practice. There will be many days during which you will not make any money, and there will be days when you will lose money. The idea is that there will be many more days that you *do* make money. Nevertheless, several very important things did happen on this day.

You now have a schedule and some structure. This is a key ingredient for the successful solo lawyer. You can't lie in bed with nowhere to go and nothing to do. Now you have something to do: get business and build your law firm.

7 Marketing: HOW TO GET AND KEEP CLIENTS

Now you have your office, your phones, your copy machine, your mentors, your business cards, your trust account, your checks printed, and … no business. What do you do? How do you get clients, and how do you keep them? My concern about teaching you how to get clients is that you may have them before you know what to do with them!

With the schedule you designed above, you'll be getting out of the house to meet clients. Meeting people is simply the key to getting business. I like to go out for breakfast. I suggest that you, depending on your preferred area of specialty, find places where potential clients of that nature will be. Now, I realize this sounds a little like I am asking you to be a prostitute in a fancy hotel lobby, but think about it: if I were writing a book about being a successful prostitute, I would suggest looking for wealthy, single men who are from out of town, and I would tell you to go to the bar of the fanciest hotel in the area late at night. Since you are reading this book, I presume you want to be a successful lawyer and will be looking for clients. So, where are they?

If you are looking to do family law cases, you might want to have your coffee at the Starbucks near a private school, early in the morning when parents are returning from dropping off kids. You might want to have coffee at the coffee shop across the street from the family law courthouse the next day. It just puts you in the place where your potential clients might be.

For almost a decade, I ate my breakfast in the same hotel dining room. Who did I meet or see there, besides other lawyers? The busboys and waiters. Each and every one of them got my card (with my cell phone number handwritten on the back because each of them was so special). I knew their names and the names of their kids. These busboys and waiters became my clients, as did their friends and their families. Each meal probably cost me more than it would have if I had eaten at home, but they got me out and about and, more importantly, they got me clients.

GOLDEN RULE: ALWAYS ALWAYS ALWAYS HAVE BUSINESS CARDS WITH YOU.

Take two things away from this section. Well, three, really. One is to always have business cards on you. I still run out of them by the end of the day and curse myself. Carry them in your wallet, in the small pocket of your jacket, and in your car. Never, ever be without one. If you are, get the card of your new contact or his name and number and send him your card the next day. Always do this.

When you take the card of a person you meet, write on the back of the card where you met them and some note about him or her to remind you. When you return to your computer or Blackberry, immediately input the information.

GOLDEN RULE: EACH CONTACT YOU MAKE MUST BE SAVED AND RECORDED.

Inputting this information is gold. First, it will help you remember who the person is and when you met him or her. Second, you are building your contact database. People you have met may one day become your clients or refer clients to you.

GOLDEN RULE: EVERYBODY YOU MEET IS A POTENTIAL CLIENT.

Everybody is a potential client. Every person you meet is a potential referral source. Treat everybody, every day, as though that person can and will send you cases. Let me give you some incredible real-life examples.

You learned about the busboy referral source earlier; I guess that one sounded obvious. But can you imagine a professor from law school sending you a case? Or their secretaries or staff? Make sure they all know that you are on your own.

How about a hairdresser? I was getting a haircut about a week after I became a lawyer. As I was reading *People* magazine, the lady cutting my hair was telling me about some kind of circumcision her son had had.

It's not that I had anything against circumcisions or her son; I was just far more interested in the celebrity gossip I was reading. So, at the end of the haircut, the lady said to me, "What do you think?"

I said, "Needs to be shorter on the sides."

She said, "No, about my son's circumcision."

Since I hadn't listened much, I said, "That's too bad."

"Well, aren't you a lawyer? Can't you help me?"

I thought to myself, "*I guess I am a lawyer, and maybe I can help him. But what do I really know at this point? I have only been a lawyer for a few days.*" Truthfully, not knowing what medical malpractice was or how to handle a medical malpractice case (there were no courses on it at the University of Miami), I figured I could bootstrap this kid's bad circumcision into a job interview. I thought I could perhaps use it as leverage to get an appointment with a lawyer and say, "Look, I have this case, and you could hire me and get the case, too."

Sadly, I did not even know what kind of lawyer would handle a case like that. I went to see, I am embarrassed to tell you, a divorce lawyer and a commercial lawyer to discuss the case. They gave me the name of one of the biggest medical malpractice lawyers in town. I met with him. He had a huge office and was by far the most likeable of all the lawyers I had met by then. He was a little guy with a huge smile and a reputation for being a real winner.

He took one look at me and my client (I had brought the boy and his father to the meeting) and said he could not help but that "Spencer could do a great job." In other words, he did not want me or the case. But he said I could do a great job.

Truthfully, I do not think I even had a contract with the client or had ever seen a client contract. As I walked out of the lawyer's huge office, I shook my head, wondering how the hell I could do a great job for the kid. I went back to my apartment and sat there and looked at my law books laying on the floor, big textbooks I had spent the last three years highlighting and schlepping to my classes.

I looked at my phone. No messages. I looked at the television. I looked in the mirror and said, "Fuck it," words that were later quoted in a front-page story about the case and how it came to be.

I called one of my law professors and asked her if she could meet me. She agreed, and when I arrived, I asked her how to start a medical malpractice case. She looked at me like I had asked her how to land a plane on an aircraft carrier. She directed me to the law library.

I found some books on medical malpractice, but trying to get through them was like reading the owner's manual for a water heater: I could not get through the first page. I looked around at the kids studying and stressing about being prepared for class. I wanted to tell them what was happening to me, but I was too embarrassed.

I called up the lawyer I had just gone to see. He was out or did not take my call. I asked for his assistant. She was afraid to give me any advice, but she suggested I speak to one of his young associates. I met with an associate and told him what I was doing or trying to do. He gave me a ten-minute seminar on how medical malpractice worked.

Most of it flew over my head, except the part about writing a letter to the hospital to see if we could resolve the case.

I had never written a lawyer demand letter before. That was another thing not taught at my law school. I wish I still had the letter, as I am sure if I saw it today, it would make me laugh. I had no office, so I used the P.O. Box address that I had had since college. I basically told the hospital that I was the lawyer of this boy who had had a bad circumcision and that he wanted to get paid money for it.

A week later, the phone rang, and it was someone from the hospital calling me to discuss it. They wanted to meet the boy and, I guess, see the "damage." I arranged it.

I called the associate and told him what was happening. He asked me what my expert's opinion was. *My expert? I need an expert on circumcisions?* He gave me the name of an urologist. I called the doctor up and explained what I needed. The urologist generously agreed to see the boy. He wrote a letter saying that the circumcision had fused to the head of the boy's penis. The doctor told me that he did a lot of work with the law firm that had referred me to him and that medical malpractice cases were very lucrative but also very expensive for lawyers. He suggested that I just send any cases I might get to this law firm rather than handling them myself. I told him I had tried but they did not want the case.

I next sent the doctor's letter to the representative from the hospital. After seeing the kid, they offered some money. I called the associate to ask his advice. He was not there. I called the lawyer whom I had met before and told him what was happening. He said to tell them something that I have used on many cases over the years: "To avoid the negative publicity associated with the case, you may want to resolve it." It has been a subtle—and sometimes not very subtle—tool that I have used to resolve many real cases and help me build my practice. Publicity, media, and just plain talking about what I do have been far more important and valuable marketing tools than TV ads for me.

In response to my suggestion, the hospital's offer went up another five thousand dollars, and the case settled. I thought I was a genius. I had literally handled my first case from my apartment.

I took my fee and used it to rent my very first law office. It was furnished. The cost of the office for the first month was two hundred dollars, as it had stood empty for thirteen years and the landlord was happy to get something for it. I call it an office, but it was really a storage room.

Once I moved into the building, things changed. The parking attendant soon became a client. The secretaries on my floor soon became clients. Every lawyer in the building knew me. One did real estate closings, another did wills; one did criminal cases, and another did immigration. I became friends with all of them. They were older. They drank and smoked, and they were going through the mid-life crises of forty-year-old lawyers. I started to drink and smoke with them— perhaps too much. I asked them questions, borrowed their forms, and got referrals for their junk cases.

Soon, I needed help. I couldn't type, and I couldn't research very well. I figured I could settle any case I had with the "negative publicity" phrase. Some I could settle, but most I could not.

The first case I could not settle came to me from Marco Rojas. I had coffee with him one day next to the courthouse. He was my age and was working for an international law firm on Brickell Avenue. He told me that his clients were from Uruguay; I did not know where that was. They had been injured at Disney World—that place I knew. Could I help them?

Of course I could. With no Internet or Skype, I found a law firm in Uruguay to help me communicate with them. I cannot remember how much I agreed to pay them, but it was a chunk. I also had to pay Marco a referral fee. I never thought in a million years we would end up going to trial. I thought I would write a letter, they would offer some money, and it would be over before happy hour at the bar across the street.

I was wrong. Disney responded by saying that my clients had signed a release in the hospital and that there was no case. I reported this back to my colleagues in Uruguay, and they responded that the clients had never signed any release. I asked Disney to send me a copy. They did, and it was in English. My clients, who only spoke Spanish, said they had no idea what they had signed. I let Disney know this. They told me, "Too bad," and the game was on.

I found a lawyer who had recently sued Disney. I met him and asked him if he wanted to work on the case with me, which meant, *Could I refer it to him?* He said no; he would never again take a Disney case. I think he had won his case but lost it on appeal or vice versa. I cannot remember. He did give me copies of his forms, however. I copied them and got help from David Vogel, my landlord's secretary. (David ultimately went to law school at UM and is now a great probate lawyer who works with me on many of my cases.)

I somehow thought if I sued Disney they would immediately want to settle. Instead, probably because they smelled enormous inexperience on my side, they decided to fight me. The lawyer they assigned looked and sounded just like Matlock. He was an Orlando lawyer, so he dressed differently than I had seen lawyers dress in my area. He did not answer phone calls and was never available to meet me or speak to me. He did all of his talking in front of the judge.

He set hearings, giving me just a day to get from Miami to Orlando. He would cancel them after I arrived. He knew what he was doing, and I had no clue. I was scared of him, but, unintentionally, he taught me a lot.

He was what is called, I later learned, a "technocrat"—a technical, go-by-the-rules lawyer. He would object to every possible thing if it was not technically accurate. Some lawyers do not get hung up on such things; in fact, most do not pay attention to every little detail—but not him.

The judge, as it turned out, was his former law partner and had worked for Disney. He told me this one morning in one of our first hearings. I had not slept the night before and had terrible diarrhea from nerves. The hearing was probably some nonsensical motion to dismiss something, but I took it on like it was the finals of a moot court competition. I pleaded—I remember being over the top—about the injustice of not letting my clients get to a jury. I am sure I plagiarized from every episode of *L.A. Law* and the closing argument of Paul Newman's *The Verdict*. In fact, I know I did because I rented *The Verdict* and took notes on it.

I won the hearing. I celebrated by going to Disney World with Dina, who would soon be my wife. After enjoying a pizza and a pitcher of beer upon arrival, I noticed that the check came with the tip amounts in Spanish. The garbage cans had Spanish words on them. There was Spanish in places where Disney wanted people to understand what they were doing—just not on the release they had provided my clients.

The case ended up costing me every cent I had. I met a banker during my Disney case who spoke with me about my practice and said he helped lawyers who needed lines of credit. I could not understand why I would ever need a line of credit. If I did not have the money, why would I put it into a case?

I got back to Miami and practiced "Door Law," which was working on whatever else came through the door: traffic tickets for the girls down the hall, and landlord-tenant disputes about the security deposits for the parking attendants. I got referrals from the guys in the buildings. I learned that if I paid the referral fees to them before I got the full amount from my clients, I might never have any money. Some of the guys waived the referrals; others asked me for gifts instead. One, may he rest in peace, said he would rather have a lamp and actually took me to the lamp store to buy it for him.

Tod Aronovitz, who later went on to be the president of the Florida Bar, would not take a referral fee. Instead, I bought him and his late wife tickets to the opera. He never referred me another case, and I joked with him often that the tickets to the opera might have actually been less of a gift and more of a punishment.

I turned down personal injury work; I did not want to be a personal injury lawyer. After Hurricane Andrew, there were many cases of people getting injured because of downed signal indicators. I rejected them. Instead, I took a bunch of cases against contractors who had defrauded homeowners. I charged very little and ended up in arbitration on those cases. I loved it. I liked being in court. I liked arguing and fighting and talking. I guess I liked the audience. However, I did not like the paperwork, the writing, or the research.

One case I had involved a houseboat that was considered a health hazard by the City of Miami. The case was my first bench trial, and I lost. I have since become good friends with the attorney who represented the city. My clients wanted to appeal, and we did. I had no idea how to handle an appeal. One of the lawyers I worked out with at the gym told me his wife was an appellate attorney. I went to meet her.

Patrice Talisman was a lot like Tina Fey. She was very pretty and could make you laugh, but at the same time, you knew you were in the presence of someone far smarter than you would ever be. I asked her if she had some forms I could follow for the appeal. She did, and she even agreed to review my brief after I was done. She worked with me on virtually every one of my cases since. I argued the appeal before the Third District Court of Appeal, the same court in which I had spent that dreadful summer while in law school. I lost. Sadly, Patty suddenly passed away in 2009 and I miss her greatly.

About two years after I filed the Disney case, it was called to trial. I had absolutely no idea how to try a case. I called one of my mentors and sat through one of his trials. I asked another mentor and sat through his. I took notes. I was panicking.

My mentors, Arno Kutner and Ken Bush, told me about a lawyer in Wyoming named Gerry Spence who had made some videos about how to try a case. Arno lent me the tapes. I watched them over and over again and have since seen this actually portrayed in a movie where a character does the same thing: watches Gerry's tapes before trial.

The tapes my mentor gave me were on Voir Dire, jury selection, and the opening statement. When I got to Orlando, I basically recited the script from the tapes. That got me a jury and to opening statements.

The news cameras were waiting for me outside the courtroom because it was a very unusual event to have a case against Disney in Orlando. At the time, it was like suing the Pope in Vatican City. One of the people who watched the news that night was a former Disney employee who had witnessed the entire incident. She, as it turned out, would be my first witness.

The case went on for a week. When time for closing statements rolled around on Friday morning, I panicked. I realized the day before that I did not know how to do a closing argument. There was no Gerry Spence tape on that. Late Thursday night, I called the lawyer who had recommended the Spence videos and cried that I was going to lose the case. I was exhausted and scared.

Ken and Arno spent a few hours on the phone with me and told me what to do. I did it, and I won. Thank God I won that first trial, because I am not sure I would be writing this book if I had not. I know this because I know of more than one lawyer who lost their first cases and never tried another, some give up practicing completely.

I have since lost many cases. In fact, I have lost more cases—many more cases—than I have won. So, why would you read a book by a lawyer who has lost so many cases? Because this is not a book about winning cases; this is a book about making your own law firm.

GOLDEN RULE: YOU WIN EVEN BY LOSING CASES.

What? How do you win by losing a case? There are a lot of lawyers out there. For a variety of reasons, only a small percentage will actually file a lawsuit on a case. Some will think it's too much work, they don't know how, it's too expensive, or they are afraid, and the list goes on. Others will file a lawsuit and do nothing with it. It will sit in their office file cabinets for months or years with little or no activity until one day they settle or get dismissed for lack of prosecution. A smaller number of lawyers will file a lawsuit but move a case erratically. With my Disney case, I moved it—but really I had no idea how or why I was moving it. Smaller still is the number of lawyers who can move a case with precision and direction, who know how and when to apply pressure and when to lighten up.

The smallest percentage of all lawyers, perhaps less than five percent, actually can take the case to trial and go all the way. I fall into that group, but there is an even more elite group than that: lawyers like Ervin Gonzalez who can go all the way and win a case most of the time. I do not pretend to be such a lawyer, but being in the top five percent means that ninety-five percent of the time, my cases will settle and settle for a reasonable amount. The defense bar and the insurance companies they represent know if they do not pay my clients, I will go all the way—even if I will lose.

So, I do not mind losing a case. I tell everyone about it. I brag about it because I want the world to know that I try cases and that if they do not settle with me I will see them at trial—for better or worse.

GOLDEN RULE: YOUR REPUTATION IS MARKETING, AND MARKETING IS EVERYTHING.

You can get new clients from existing clients, from lawyers, from your hairdresser, and from the parking attendant. Always be aware of that.

GOLDEN RULE: DRESS LIKE A LAWYER.

My mom recently said to me when she saw me running to the airport to catch a flight to Los Angeles, "Why are you so dressed up to fly? Why not wear sweats and be comfortable?"

"Because, Mom," I replied, "I never know who I am going to meet. The lady sitting next to me on the flight might be the relative of a famous person who just lost a loved one because of medical malpractice, or she might need an immigration attorney for her uncle. You just never know."

GOLDEN RULE: ACT LIKE AN ESQ. AND NOT AN S.O.B.

Oh, how I cringed when I saw my friend, a very successful lawyer, toss his Porsche keys to the parking attendant and say, "Park it up front," without even looking him in the face. The waiter came, and my friend spoke into the menu and then handed it to the waiter without even looking up after he ordered.

My friend is rich and successful and one of the best lawyers in town. He worked for some of the best, and maybe that is why he acts the way he does. Maybe he does not even notice; few of us ever really see what other people see in us.

But he acts the way most of the lawyers I know act: snobby jerks to the average guy. When they are in front of a jury, they are all apple pie and ice cream. But what do I know? They are all driving Turbo Porsches and summering in their second homes in Gstaad or St. Barts.

The point I am making is this: please, please do not act like a jerk when you are out there. Act kindly and generously to the staff at your five-star hotel and when in line at 7-Eleven. I always pass out business cards, too, and almost inevitably someone will need a lawyer for something. Who knows? Just be humble.

GOLDEN RULE: JOIN GROUPS, GO OUT, AND BE SOCIAL.

I am really not great at this part. I do not really like group settings. I am a one-on-one type of guy, but some people are great in groups. Join the local PETA, Gay and Lesbian Chamber of Commerce, French Film Club—whatever you like and enjoy doing, just join that group.

Make sure the other members know you are a lawyer and what kind of law you practice. Offer a discount to members of the organization for fees on legal consultations. Spend some time and energy participating in the groups, and have fun doing it.

8 WHEN WILL I KNOW IF I HAVE MADE IT?

It sounds obvious, but unless you know where you want to be, you may already be there and not know it. Many of you reading this only have the same vague and delusional idea of what a lawyer really does that I had when I first decided to go to law school. I envisioned life would be like Arnie Becker's (my favorite character on *L.A. Law*, portrayed by Corbin Bernsen). I figured I would get up early, work out in my beachfront manse, jump in the pool, have a protein smoothie, put the top down on my Porsche, and drive to my downtown law firm. Waiting for me there would be gorgeous secretaries, clients, and other lawyers who were all amazed at the ease with which I glided through life. Once in a while, I would go to court, and somewhere in the next forty-five minutes, between commercials, I would have done an opening and a closing and would be back at the office before the credits rolled, basking in my brilliance and smoking a cigar with the older lawyer who was my mentor/surrogate father.

Hey, come on. Give me a break. I was a twenty-year-old college student with no idea about anything, so I am hoping that I am not the only one who felt this way. I know that in the year I applied to law school (1988) UM Law had the largest number of applicants in its history. Many thought it was because of *L.A. Law*. Ironically, I met Corbin Bernsen and we became friends. He was astonished to learn of his influence on me and so many other people's career choices.

The point I am making is that the goal or destination I had at twenty was at least measurable. In other words, I would have said in 1988 that I had arrived once:

1. I had a Porsche.

2. I had a beachfront manse.

3. I was in court.

4. I had an office in a big building.

5. I was surrounded by beautiful secretaries, clients, and lawyers.

6. I had an adoring mentor/father figure to smoke cigars with each night while sipping Armagnac.

Foolish, perhaps, but tangible, for sure. Of course, my idea of having made it has changed significantly in the last twenty-one years, and so will yours. Go through the following exercise so you can figure out where you are and where you want to be. Before you answer the following questions, close your eyes for at least ten deep breaths and focus on a vision of yourself as a lawyer.

Now finish this sentence: "I will have made it as a lawyer when _____."

1. I am living in a _____.

2. I am driving _____.

3. I am in court _____.

4. My office is _____.

5. I live with _____.

6. I work ___ hours a day.

7. I work ____ hours a week.

8. I spend ____ days a year on vacation.

9. I spend my vacations doing _____.

10. I make $_____ a year.

11. I save $_____ a year.

12. I retire when I _____.

X _____ _Aspiring Young Lawyer_

Date: _____

Time: _____

Place: _____

Sign and date this form once you have completed it, and indicate the time and place you came to this vision. Then print and save it.

For me, the exact amount of money I made was secondary to the lifestyle I wanted. And things have changed. Some years ago, I wanted to live in the courtroom; now that is much less important. Some years ago, you could not have paid me to take a vacation; I simply would not go. Others I knew did not want to come back from vacation.

Things change. So will you. In fact, you may not even be practicing in five years, but if you are, I promise you that your vision will be different. I suggest that you docket one year from the date of signing the vision and look at it every year. Like when you use a GPS, you may have to make minor tweaks and turns to stay on your path.

Many people have advised me to have five- and ten-year plans. All that would be great if:

1. I wanted the same thing in five years that I want today.

2. I had any clue where I am today.

3. I had any idea how to get to where I think I want to be in five years.

Once you can come up with the yearly goal, take another ten deep breaths with your eyes closed and then complete the following statements:

1. To live in a _____, I have to _____.

2. To drive a _____, I have to _____.

3. To spend ___ days in court, I have to _____.

4. To have my office _____, I have to _____.

5. To live with _____, I have to _____.

6. To work ___ hours a day, I have to _____ _____ _____.

7. To work ___ hours a week, I have to _____ _____ _____.

8. To spend ___ days a year on vacation, I have to _____ _____ _____.

9. To spend my vacations doing _____, I have to _____ _____.

10. To make $_____ a year, I have to _____ _____ _____.

11. To save $_____ a year, I have to _____
   _____
   _____.

12. To retire when I am _____, I have to _____
   _____
   _____.

X _____ *Aspiring Young Lawyer*

Date: _____

Time: _____

Place: _____

Print this out and sign and date it. Keep it taped to your bathroom mirror, on the inside lid of your briefcase, and as the desktop screensaver on your computer.

9 MONEY AND THINGS

More than a couple of you may be reading this because you want to find out how to get rich being a lawyer, how to acquire money to buy things, have stuff, and show off. I am sorry to tell you this late in the book that I really have no clue about that.

I really do not think you can get rich being a lawyer. Most lawyers I know are not rich. Sure, they may look that way, but that is all part of this foolish delusion. Of course, there are the exceptions: those few who have their own jets, villas in Tuscany, professional sports teams, and enough money to never work again. Ironically, all the lawyers I know who have all those things (and I know a few of them very well) do not do their jobs for the money. They do it because they love the job, and they work much harder than you would think anyone with that kind of money really would or should.

Gerry Spence, who is the greatest lawyer who ever lived and has achieved a degree of financial reward in excess of the wealth of hundreds of lawyers combined, tried many of his cases for free. He also established a not-for-profit school on his own ranch to teach lawyers around the country how to be better lawyers. The Trial Lawyers College costs him money, but he created it. I was privileged to be one of his students and then spent months with him on his book tours.

The greatest gift he gave me was demanding that I be myself. So, to you I say, if your primary goal in becoming a lawyer or in starting your own firm is to get rich, do not do it. Go into business instead. What kind of business? Well, that is for another book by another author. I do not have a clue.

I do make money being a lawyer, but I am not rich. Sure, I live in a nice house and drive a nice car, but still that does not mean I am rich. People are often shocked or disappointed to hear this. Clients want to believe, at least in Miami, that their lawyers are superrich. Young lawyers who meet me want to think that they are taking advice from a rich lawyer. The problem is that people confuse being a rich with being good lawyer or even a good person.

For years after spending time with Gerry, I battled with thinking that being a great lawyer (my goal for many years) and making money were completely inapposite. Really, how could I fight for my clients with all my heart and soul if I was worried about how much money I was making?

I never settled cases back then. Instead, I ended up trying and losing many cases that should have been settled. Back then, I never thought about the financial equation of practicing law. I had no idea how much money I made or how much cases cost to litigate; I just kept going to the courthouse.

Somehow, I made money, but with this blasé attitude I came close to going broke a number of times. I lost hundreds of thousands of dollars on cases that were losers. I guess I did not care how difficult the case was. I guess I had too much faith in juries. I guess I was just young and passionate about justice.

Around 2004, my wife had a health crisis that required a lot more medical care than my health insurance would cover. I did not have the cash to pay for it. I refinanced the house, but it was not enough. I asked for money from her dad. He reluctantly gave me very very little, but not enough. I asked for money from my parents, and they both generously helped me as much as they could. In the middle of all this, I tried a case and asked for way too much money from the jury—a classic and stupid mistake. Forgive me, Gerry. I am sure the jury could see through me, and they came back with a defense verdict. I was in big trouble. Then my associate quit. Actually, she went home that night and never came back.

Then I got sick. Literally, the day my wife came home from the hospital, I was in intensive care, dying. Something (I guess from stress) had just burst in my stomach, and I was bleeding to death. My parents came to the hospital, along with my wife and my rabbi. I never thought I was going to die, but they did.

In the midst of this, my receptionist quit, John Kerry lost to George W. Bush, and Floridians agreed to pass a constitutional amendment limiting attorneys' fees in medical malpractice cases to just ten percent. I guessed I could handle losing some staff if I could not pay them. I could have been evicted from my space, but fortunately, I was not. My landlord hung on. I suppose I could have filed for bankruptcy.

But, putting all this aside, I want to talk about the worst-case scenario for me or any other solo practitioner. What if I had been evicted and lost all my staff? What if I had actually had to file bankruptcy? *What if?*

The point is that I started my practice with nothing but a passionate and desperate desire to be a lawyer. I often fantasize about what I would do if I had to start all over again now. Where would I go, and how would I do it? I think I would take my ten best files, find a small corner in my apartment or a small storage room in someone else's office, and start all over again. As I suggested earlier in the book, I would ask lawyers if they had work for me in exchange for some space.   I would pass out business cards. I would go to breakfasts; I would meet people. I think—no, I truly believe—that I could be back on my feet within a few months to a year.

That is the true beauty of owning your own law firm. We sole practitioners do not need anybody but ourselves to be lawyers. What freedom! What a blessing!

10 A WORD ABOUT STAYING ETHICAL

Without question, there will be many opportunities to make ethical mistakes as a solo practitioner. I am assuming that you are in fact an ethical and well-intentioned lawyer, so I will not spend any time or paper counseling you not to steal clients' money, lie to the court, or hide evidence. If you need me to tell you about that, then you need more than this book.

I am concerned about the ethical mistakes you might make because you simply do not know any better. Again, another failure of law schools is that if they teach ethics at all, it is in the form of some abstract nonsense that will mean little or nothing to you when you open your doors. My law school ethics course was taught by a well-meaning South African exchange teacher who had never practiced law in Florida (nor, I assume, in South Africa). It was completely useless.

Each state has its own rules on ethics. The Florida Bar even has an ethics hotline you can call to get an opinion, anonymously, on any ethical dilemma. Even with that, you are bound to make some mistakes that can be distractions at best and at worst can cost you your law license.

Following are a few rules that apply in Florida. I suggest you assume they apply in your state as well until you take the time to find out.

You will probably be as surprised as I was to learn that you cannot share a fee with a non-lawyer. If a client, relative, friend, or employee refers you a case, you cannot give them any money as a thank you, reward, or commission. You simply cannot.

In addition, there are certain kinds of cases in which you cannot even pay a referral fee to another lawyer. In Florida, this includes criminal and divorce cases. In Florida, there are also limits on how much of a referral fee you can give to another lawyer in a legitimate referable case. Some less-than-scrupulous lawyers may try to take advantage of your inexperience and desperation and ask you for a greater percentage of the fee than they are entitled to. Exceptions exist for certain types of co-counsel arrangements and with court approval.

There are limits on how much of a fee you can take on a contingency fee case. I have had several clients offer to give me more that the bar-regulated percentages if I would just take their cases. There are also specific languages and contracts that must be used on contingency fee agreements in Florida. I am sure your state has similar ones. You need to get copies and use them.

It is unethical to not return a client's call. Yes, really. So return all of their calls or fire the client.

There are rules on advertisements, business cards, announcements, websites, office sharing, and just about everything that governs the practice of law that most people do not know and end up finding out only when it's too late. You may ask, *Who cares if I have an advertisement or business card that does not comply with the letter of the ethics code?* You will be surprised when you start making enemies as fast as you start making friends. Being a lawyer is not a real popularity contest.

People will be jealous of the guts you had to open your own office. Opposing counsel will try to distract you with bar complaints and contempt motions. I have had it all and then some at the same time. Disgruntled clients will grieve about you to the Bar because you do not meet their expectations, return their every phone call, or do the unethical things they may demand of you. Some will do it just to extort money from you. Get ready.

Bottom line: You will get Bar complaints. You will be sued. Be prepared.

GOLDEN RULE: NEVER DO ANYTHING THAT MIGHT JEOPARDIZE YOUR TICKET.

Never put yourself in harm's way. It is simply not worth it.

GOLDEN RULE: KEEP MUM WITH YOUR STAFF ABOUT ETHICAL ISSUES.

If you ever do something unethical—whether intentionally or not—*do not ever tell your staff.* You never want a staff member to have something to hold over your head. They can extort you. They can make your life miserable. They can and will tell their friends, who might extort you themselves, even if your staff does not.

GOLDEN RULE: DO NOT DO ANYTHING UNETHICAL WITH A NON-LAWYER.

Non-lawyers will offer to be runners or give you kickbacks or pay you in cash for things, which might be very tempting, especially when cash flow has dried up. Please be careful. They have little or nothing to lose—but you do.

What if a clinic, court reporter, or process server offers you cash for each client you send them? Little or nothing will happen to them. You, however, might become their slave for the next thirty years as they extort money from you for their silence. Or, perhaps worse, you might lose your license.

If there is no way to get in touch with your state bar for an opinion, you can always ask your lawyer for his opinion. I do not know how great a defense it is, but having a legal opinion about your idea is probably better than just guessing about whether you are right. Unlike most businesses, the practice of law has some of the most stringent and often senseless restrictions. Welcome to owning your own law firm.

What happens if you make a mistake? You will—it's just a matter of time. You can try to hedge your losses by getting malpractice insurance; however, most solo practitioners and young lawyers are impossible to insure or impossibly expensive to insure because of the risk.

I was uninsurable for my first several years because of inexperience. Imagine the risk of a personal injury lawyer with less than five years' experience, who was working with no support staff, without a conflict of interest check in place, and with no calendar backup and no clue? Forget it.

After a few years, I eventually became insured and remained so for about the following ten years. When I went through the financial trauma discussed in the previous chapter, legal malpractice insurance became a luxury I thought I could live without, along with my Jaguar convertible and my wife's Land Rover.

I also, somewhat overconfidently or even cockily, did not think I would ever make any really big mistakes that I could not resolve or cover on my own. So I went "bare" for about two years until I finally made a real mistake.

By the way, any mistake made by your staff, receptionist, bookkeeper, associates, law clerks, or you counts entirely as your mistake. As the solo practitioner, there is no one else to blame when something gets lost, docketed incorrectly, or misunderstood. The more distracted you are in running around trying to be a lawyer and the more dependent you are on your staff, the more likely it is that things will happen. It is not only human to err, it is inevitable. And I really fucked one up.

I had no insurance, and the potential loss to my client and ultimately to me was in the millions—perhaps tens of millions. I will not bore you with the details, but the nearly perfect storm of shit had formed over my head.

It was a Friday night around 5:00 PM when I finally realized and began to understand what had happened. I could not stand up and was sitting in my reception area as I watched my staff turn off the lights and go home for the weekend. One in particular smiled at me and said, "I guess you have got this under control. I'll see you on Monday."

The first thing I did was call the client, who, up until this happened, had been perhaps one of the most difficult clients I had ever represented. He would call almost daily and require hours of my time to listen to his rants. At times, I had almost fired him as a client because he was so time and energy consuming. Now I was regretting that I had not listened to myself.

I told this young man late on Friday afternoon that I had made a mistake. I was honest and sincere. I told him that I would do everything I could to make it right, and that if I could not make it right, I would spend the rest of my life working to make sure he was made right. I also told him he had the right to seek another lawyer and that, if he did, I would do everything I could to help his new lawyer while still trying to resolve the case. He believed me, yet I suspect he did speak to some other lawyers.

Then I called the lawyer who had referred me the case. He was home already and relaxing. I told him that through an error of mine I had potentially damaged the case he had referred me. In Florida, a referral lawyer is responsible for the mistakes that the lawyer to whom he refers the case makes, so he had exposure too. Rather than yell and scream at me, he said that he would stick by me until the issue was resolved and that anything owed to the client he would be good for too. I started to breathe.

Two of my secretaries stayed with me until I had the strength to drive home. On the drive home, I reflected that less than a day before, only a few hours earlier, I had felt better than I had in years. In fact, I have a photo taken of me the day before this happened, and I look like a million bucks. I have never looked better since.

My stomach pains suddenly reappeared. I ignored them.

On Monday I hired a lawyer to help me, and another, and another.

I spoke to my trusted friend, Patrice Talisman, who ran to my office to help me strategize. I called my mentor, Ken Bush. I told all of my friends and some people who were not my friends. Yes, it was embarrassing, but I needed advice, and I wanted to share the mistake with those I cared about so they did not make a similar mistake themselves.

Had I had legal malpractice insurance, I would have turned the whole thing over to some drone at a big insurance defense firm who probably would not have cared about what happened to me. His concern would have been the insurance policy that insured me. I doubt he would have stayed up nights and weekends trying to figure out a way to get me out of my mess. But I did.

Never being very good at legal research, I miraculously came across a single case that ultimately proved to be the key in unraveling my mistake. The judge agreed with my case, as did the appellate court. Ultimately, my client got paid, and I gladly paid all those lawyers who had helped me, including the referral lawyer. I had not just dodged a bullet—I had dodged a nuclear bomb.

What would have happened if I had lost? I would have just had to start all over again, and I know I could have, because I have before. Welcome to owning your own law firm.

So, should you have legal malpractice insurance? Yes, and not for the reasons expressed above. You should have it so you don't have to worry about losing it all if—rather, when—you make a mistake. The worry was more damaging to my well-being than the loss would have been. It made me sick.

You should also get malpractice insurance for another, equally important reason. If your mistake does in fact cost your client money, you need to be able to make things right to him. You cannot let your mistake injure your client. That, to me, is unethical.

11 STAYING HEALTHY

Solo practice is a recipe for excess. It's stressful beyond just being a lawyer; you are running a business too. The opportunities to meet lawyers after work for a drink or two or three can easily turn into a nasty habit.

Those with addictive personalities like my own are more likely to have a problem. I do not drink or smoke now, but I did in the past, and I had trouble controlling it. The more I smoked and drank, the more I wanted to smoke and drink. And I am not alone. I smoked cigars, and the more I smoked, the more I wanted (or thought I wanted) to smoke. I would spend the first ten minutes of each morning coughing my lungs out into the sink.

Food has been a problem for me my whole life. In many ways, it is my drug of choice. Tough day in the office? Hide your Häagen-Dazs. I have in my closet at least four different sizes of suits. I get really skinny and really fat. I am like Oprah.

You must take care not to fall into the typical trap that derails so many of us lawyers, especially the solo practitioner.

I hate going to the gym, so I had to hire a personal trainer. That forces me to show up and work out for at least thirty minutes or so. I am embarrassed to spend the money and share with you this weakness, but it is true. I simply do not have the discipline or desire to work out. This is my expensive little trick, and it works.

See a doctor at least once a year, if not more often. It is much easier to prevent an illness than cure one. Stress can and will make you sick, if not kill you. I know. I recommend that you see a doctor who is more than just an HMO drone who will only give you a ten-minute physical after you have waited for three hours. Find someone who will actually listen to what is happening in your life and is willing to order all the diagnostic tests he would like you to have if money or insurance were not an issue.

Feeling sad or blue? See a shrink. The stress and loneliness of owning your own law firm can be overwhelming for you and your family. Dealing with issues before they become irreversible is essential.

Bottom line: all the hard work, seminars, and marketing will not mean anything if you do not take care of yourself mentally, physically, spiritually, and emotionally.

I have met many lawyers who will spend ten thousand dollars on a watch but will not have a physical examination by a doctor, get their eyes checked, have a single blood test, or even get a massage. You are the engine, the starting quarterback, and the star of your show on which so many depend. Your family, staff, and clients all depend on your ability to show up tomorrow morning, ready to rock. The fact that this section is near the end of the book is in no way meant to suggest that taking care of your health is any less important than finding the right secretary or office. It is, in many ways, the single most important piece of the puzzle.

12 QUITTING

You sure did not buy a book about how to quit the practice of law, did you? Want to hear a secret? I have wanted to quit many, many times. Once I wanted to stop and open a bagel bakery. I even went and interviewed for a job at a bagel place that I thought had the right stuff. I did not even get the job.

Near the end of 2006, after fifteen years of practice, I decided to quit and move to Italy. My wife wanted us to move to Dubai. Her dad said Romania. My father suggested the Cayman Islands.

What would I do? How would I make a living? What would happen to my practice? Who cared? At times, I have been so disenchanted with the practice of law and practicing on my own that I could not face another day in the office. Sometimes, I was so bored and tired of hearing the woes of the little old lady who slipped on a banana peel in Wal-Mart that I wanted to slit my wrists.

It's completely normal and probably inevitable that at some point that you will get burned out. So, first, I want you to know that it is completely honorable to quit. Honestly, you would be doing yourself, your family, and certainly your clients a favor not to labor through some case or trial if you are not really into it.

But then what do you do?

GOLDEN RULE: PREVENTING BURNOUT IS MUCH EASIER THAN FIXING IT.

Before the signs and symptoms of burnout surface, there are a number of things you can do to avoid it. But first, let's consider the signs:

1. Dread at the thought of getting out of bed.
2. Dread at the thought of going to work.
3. Finding excuses for not doing things that your job requires.
4. Coming in late.
5. Taking long lunches.
6. Finding yourself spending time surfing the Internet instead of working.
7. Continuing trials, mediations, and depositions so that you do not have to do them.
8. Not taking client calls.
9. Weight gain.
10. Overconsumption of alcohol.
11. Finding someone or something to spend your time with that is interfering with your activities as a lawyer.
12. Not caring about the outcome of your clients' cases.
13. Boredom.

For me, things started to go downhill in 2005. I started to get really bored. I started to think that each case was essentially the same case with a different name. My staff was apathetic and seemed to be infected with my lethargy. I started coming in later and later. So did my staff.

I was not looking for an escape and did not even really understand what was happening to me. I was just tired of being a lawyer. I, like you, had started my journey in my junior year of college with the LSAT, then applications to law school, then law school and the bar. I started without the firm and began trying cases, making money, losing cases, losing money ... It just became so uninspiring.

So I took some time off. I did not do it intentionally. At the time, I thought I was actually refueling myself for the second half of my career, which I realize I am in now. I just decided that riding my bicycle or, in truth, racing my bicycle was a more enjoyable way to spend my days.

So that's what I did.

I also started to look at other places to live and other jobs I could do. Miami, which had begun to seem like such a dismal place, started to look a whole lot better when I started to compare it to other places to live—to live, not to visit.

The practice of law also started to look a hell of a lot more appetizing when I considered that at forty years old, I really did not know how to do anything else. I certainly didn't know how to do anything nearly as well as I knew how to be a lawyer.

Avoid burning out by making sure it never happens. Here are some strategies I have learned work:

1. Schedule days off. I mean put them in the calendar and make sure they happen. I have just now learned to actually put personal days on the calendar for the year. I have one personal day in each month on the calendar. Usually it is on a Friday, but sometimes it is in the middle of the week.

2. Schedule a vacation. Cannot afford to take a day off or a long weekend? I learned long ago that the rest and recovery you get from just a short vacation can give you an added boost of energy when you get back. I would rather take one day off a

month than two weeks off at one time. Either way, just make sure you do it.

3. Turn the Blackberry off. Anyone who has had dinner with me or has seen me drive while typing on my Blackberry and talking into the phone with the other hand will laugh or probably cry at this. But you have to turn it off. It took me nearly twenty years and many sleepless nights to learn this. I'll be lying in bed, and just out of habit or boredom, I'll turn on my Blackberry. Bam! Twenty messages, some seemingly urgent. Many of my clients now e-mail me. Referral lawyers e-mail me. My staff e-mails me. I respond, they respond, and then I cannot sleep. I start to worry, or my mind starts to race.

4. Seminars are seminars, not vacations. The Association of Intellectual Property Lawyers has an annual convention in Maui. If you go, this is not a vacation. This is work and does not count toward your time off—Maui or not.

5. Dinner with clients, referral lawyers, or experts … it all counts as work. No matter how much you like going to the watch the Miami Heat with your favorite expert, you are still on the clock, and that does not count as time off.

6. Spend time with your spouse. You calendar every minute of your day, but you do not calendar your date nights or lunches with the one you love and who loves you. Make it as important as your next hearing, and put it in your calendar.

7. Spend time with your kids. I realized when Sara turned ten that I hardly ever saw her. She was in school or with tutors. When I came home, she was asleep. I was barely seeing my baby girl at all. So now I try to have a date night with her every Tuesday night. Unfortunately, it rarely happens.

8. Do not become a different person just because you have an "Esq." at the end of your name. The Spencer I was before I started practicing rarely surfaces anymore. I hardly have belly

laughs like I did with Donald Baker in law school; we'd laugh until it hurt and we cried. I hardly see movies anymore. I do not skateboard or dance or smile a lot. I really don't. I have a serious expression or a scowl most of time. I have a weight on my shoulders that, even if it lifts for a minute or two, comes back the minute I wake up. Some may say that I have just grown up. But the truth is I am not really happy very often. A time came when I realized that I was almost never really happy at all. There was just too much stress and drama. Everything was stressful, including just taking the kids to Disney World. I was running late, had to get back for something, or had some emergency waiting for me. There was always a problem—or so I thought.

Writing this book is just such an example. It has bounced around in my head for at least ten years, but during all that time I didn't write it. I could not relax long enough to let it flow out of my head and onto the pages. I thought about where I would be the happiest when writing this book. I envisioned that a really nice and quiet hotel with great room service and clean sheets would be what I needed. And it was. I stopped taking calls from the office. I turned the Blackberry off and just let loose.

Within a day or two, I started to relax, and I produced the work you have been reading. I slept as long as I wanted and went to sleep when I was tired. I gave myself what I needed so that I could give you this book. My point is that, somewhere inside you, you know what you need to recharge yourself.

Take a minute, close your eyes, and think about this before you answer the following questions:

1. When I get stressed out and lose myself,
   I need to go to _____.

2. When I get stressed out and lose myself,
   I need to be with _____.

3. When I get stressed out and lose myself,
   I need to do _____.

Keep this posted with your notes from the other exercises in this book, and make sure that you do this at least once or twice a year, if not more. You will say to yourself, *I am fine. I cannot afford to do this, and I am tougher than that Aronfeld, anyway, with his trainers and shrinks …* Okay, you're a tough guy or gal, but I am trying to help you finish this race, not just get through the first few stages. The Tour de France has two rest days, and in creating the universe, even God took a day off. Shouldn't you?

I decided in January 2007 to give it one last chance. In doing so, I enlisted the help of some very talented advisors and coaches to help me reengineer my practice and my life. I obtained a practice advisor, the great Michael Smith, who, having listened to my story, came to my office and spent some time with me and my staff. He came to the conclusion one Saturday morning that I was going to go broke, lose my staff, or go insane if I continued to practice the way I had for the previous sixteen years.

I battled with him, cursed at him, and told him he had no idea what the practice of law was about (he is not an attorney) or the stress from my staff, family, clients, or the voice inside me that was always pushing me to be more.

He tried again on Sunday. I fought back again. He said that perhaps he was not the right guy for me and that what I needed was a shrink, maybe even some medication. I remember leaving his apartment that day to attend a wedding. I was livid. I could not sit through the ceremony, much less the lavish dinner.

I called my personal physician, Chris Renna, whom I had hired to help me with my stomach problems.

He said, "You know, the practice advisor might be right. Why not get checked out?" I went to a shrink. I poured my guts out to her about my life, my office, my marriage, and my passion for bicycle racing.

She said, "You know, I do not think you have a problem, but why not get checked out?"

She referred me to yet another specialist, who tested me for Adult Attention Deficit Disorder. I spent two days and several thousand dollars getting tested. The results came back that I have a mind that has difficulty focusing, and I am easily distracted. I am impulsive and have trouble sitting still. The doctor who tested me said that he was surprised that I was able to get through law school, much less graduate *cum laude*, with the severity of my condition. I had always known this, but I did not know there was a name for it, other than the Yiddish expression—*schpilkas*.

Let me be more specific about how my mind works: I can express myself both in speech and on the pages of this book with almost effortless abandon for hours on end. But should you ask me to organize the pages and details or count the words, I would get it wrong or get bored doing it within a minute or two.

I was recommended a trial prescription of Concerta, a medication that is given to people with AADD. I was concerned that it would make me dumb or affect my creativity or my memory or worse, make me something or someone less than I am. I also did not like the stigma attached to it. It sounded like I was nuts. In many ways, I guess I am.

But, inspired in part by my desire to be the best I can be at everything I do, I agreed to try the drug. Almost instantly (and I do not even know if that is how it is supposed to work) I started to feel better. I became able to accomplish some things in the office I never could before, like sit down and read an entire medical chart without moving around, read a book in the midst of a noisy flight, and keep from daydreaming in a seminar.

I think that the medication has worn off a little in the last few years, but I still take it. Why would I share this most intimate and embarrassing experience with you? Because I wrote this book to help people start and build their own law firms. I was weighed down for much of my life and struggled, perhaps unnecessarily, to study and retain information. This helped me. While you may not have ADD, you may have something else or perhaps nothing at all. Get checked out just to be sure.

Another thing that has helped me and that was inspired in large part by another hero of mine, Lance Armstrong, is having a team of coaches. I have had the practice adviser, Chris Akers, (a new one now who helps me in a more-detailed manner), the doctor, the shrink(s), the personal trainer, the accountant, the IT guy, and soon a marketing person. It sounds like it takes a village, and for me it does. Sure, you can get by with less; or perhaps you'll need more. Just know that you can and should look for all the help you need to make your firm a success.

13 SOCIAL NETWORKING

From the time I first started this book until its eventual publication, the importance and variety of social networking for lawyers has exploded. You see, every business has to market itself to attract and keep customers. For lawyers today, attracting and keeping clients is more complex and competitive than ever. I believe every member of my staff has both the ability and obligation to bring in business, though I know that ultimately that responsibility falls on me. If I fail, the business will fail and none of us will have a job.

This book and the subsequent book tour is, after all, a form of marketing. I not only accept that, I am a proud of it.

For most of my career, traditional lawyer advertising consisted of an old guy in front of a bookcase asking if "you have been injured in a car accident" and advising to call his office. Of course, I live and practice in Florida, and lawyer advertisement is subject to the stringent provisions of the Florida Bar. Some states seem to have no restrictions at all, and lawyer ads on TV, billboards, radio seem to be outrageous.

Traditional advertisement is expensive to produce, hard to modify, and associated with negative connotations. I have for the most part avoided it, but as my practice evolves into mass tort work, we are exploring the need to advertise on television and other mediums to acquire cases.

The new sole practitioner can still compete with some established advertisers by using the Internet. The Internet provides the creative lawyer/entrepreneur an opportunity to connect and stay connected with both existing and potential clients worldwide, essentially for free. It's called social networking. Learning how to use the networking sites wisely can increase both the lawyer and the firm's profile.

Engaging in social networking requires a willingness to surrender some personal information online to create a profile. However, people should be cautioned about revealing too much because once this information is out there, it is never coming back. Never.

Accordingly, avoid posting home addresses, children's identities, and social security and driver's license numbers. Always use your office addresses as your address, and do not post your cell phone number unless you are prepared to receive calls from anybody at any hour.

The first step in social media is deciding what you want your social media to accomplish. And be realistic. My goal is to simply give my existing contact base some top-of-the-mind awareness of what I am doing and why. I am careful to not make it seem too informal or too obvious that I am marketing. If you do not feel like you are qualified to make this kind of marketing decision, you should consult someone who is, like an ad agent or marketer.

The second step is to identify your target audience. With social networking, you can to some degree control who gets your messages by selecting the audience. Some sites even allow you to limit the demographics to geography and age.

You can use social networking sites to make announcements, such as verdicts, settlements, or that you are hiring a new receptionist. The larger the number of connections you have, the more people will be aware of your message.

What is even more interesting is that many sites are now linked to each other, meaning that a posting on Twitter can land you in Facebook or a blog. So, be aware that your message may end up going to other sites and other people that you do not necessarily control.

Here is a partial list of what is available to lawyers:

LINKEDIN

LinkedIn is the serious older brother of MySpace and Facebook and is used almost exclusively by professionals looking to promote themselves and their businesses. Basically, LinkedIn is like posting on the web your most trusted contacts and people are judged by the company they keep. People solicit others to give them recommendations to increase their "status." Currently, I have 101 LinkedIn connections. A typical announcement I can make to this group is: "Appears on the Tyra Banks Show November 3, 2009 at 4:00 PM EST discussing plastic surgery malpractice." The true value of LinkedIn lies in the groups. Presently there are over 200,000 groups, and 150 of these groups deal with lawyers. Creating a group or a subgroup of a group takes no more than five minutes and can be used as a "club within a club" to do more specific networking.

I take the position of accepting anyone who wants to be connected to me in Facebook or LinkedIn. I accept everyone on these sites since I use them as a marketing tool and have not put extremely sensitive information on my profile. For example:

Appears on the Tyra Banks Show November 3, 2009 at 4:00 PM EST discussing plastic surgery malpractice.

To see our LinkedIn information, go to: http://www.linkedin.com/in/aronfeld

TWITTER

Twitter is the shot of espresso of social marketing. It is quick and permits only short messages blasted to whoever is following you. You can also upload mini links to videos and pictures. Most businesses that use

Twitter think of it as a promotional tool to announce a promotion or drive traffic to their blog or websites.

I do not recommend directly contacting clients with social networking to discuss personal, confidential information, since I am not sure how accessible it is. Disgruntled clients can post angry tweets complaining about your service. You can monitor your name or firm by using programs like Monittor and resolve problems that you might never hear about otherwise.

To see our Twitter page, go to: http://twitter.com/aronfeld

BLOGS

With a hundred million blogs now online, you may feel as though the last thing you needs is another website. However, if you don't have a blog, you might want to reconsider. Blogs can help a lawyer establish a human connection with clients, referrals, and even potential jurors. Blogs are persona and not so "staged" as firm websites. Blogs can also help you tap into conversations with potential clients and respond immediately to trends in the law.

Setting up a blog is quick and easy. A number of blogging software applications are free, including Google's Blogger and Movable Type. Figuring out what you want your blog to say is more complicated. Don't settle for a company blog that is a simple repository for press releases and other junk. Instead, you should cultivate the image of an expert in your field and even a trusted friend.

You can think of a blog as your own soapbox or diary. Google has a number of tracking features so you can monitor your blog's visitors and activity.

To see our blog, go to: http://www.floridainjurylawyer-blog.com/

FACEBOOK

Imagine a website that will allow you to find old friends, schoolmates, or missing neighbors and then share with them photos, videos, and invitations to events. Facebook also will make suggestions based upon your profile of people who it thinks you know or should know.

Facebook can also be used to create a business presence with a very personal touch. People follow people each other on Facebook, as on Twitter. However, with Facebook there is no limit to the amount of information that can be posted or the number of people you can follow.

The biggest mistake I see some people make with Facebook is farming their content out to ghostwriters. Facebook should be a personal statement about you to your friends and connections. It can and will help you find lost contacts from high school that might now be potential referral sources.

I resisted Facebook until I found that it is hugely popular with my clients. I get responses almost immediately anytime I put something on Facebook. It is extremely easy to use, especially with a Blackberry.

To see our Facebook page, go to: http://www.facebook.com/people/Spencer-Aronfeld/567179947

EMAIL BLAST

Email blasts are basically like sending a newsletter, but on the Internet. The advantage is that it is fast, cheap, and can be linked to other content on the web such as video, photos, or surveys.

Sending email newsletters allows lawyers to stay fresh in the minds of their clients and defense counsel. There is tracking software that allows you to know how many people click on the newsletter and what they read.

However, one should be careful about buying lists of recipients or sending emails to unwanted recipients as it could result in having your IP address permanently blocked. Many email newsletters provide a feature that will minimize the chances of being deemed spam. Once you are reported as being a spammer or abusing the Internet, it will be difficult to use your email account for genuine email communications.

Want to see what our email newsletter looks like? Subscribe to it on our website: www.aronfeld.com

YOUTUBE

In 2010, we opened a YouTube channel that we constantly update. We keep the content visual and dynamic, enabling an exciting dimension to law firm marketing. Through YouTube, we can immediately provide instant information in an interesting format regarding our clients and events.

To visit our YouTube channel, go to: www.youtube.com/user/TheMiamilawyer

You should check with your state's bar regarding restrictions that may apply to the use of social media. Florida's Bar has issued some pretty tight rules as to what can and cannot be said and considers social media to be basically the same as other forms of advertisement. Here are the current Florida Bar rules, but do not rely on it even if you are in Florida, as the rules seem to change as fast as there are new social media sites.

14 EVERY LAWYER NEEDS A MENTOR

In fact lawyers need many mentors. My relationship with Gerry Spence, arguably the greatest lawyer who ever lived, started like something out of a movie.

As previously discussed, my friend and mentor, Ken Bush, and his then-partner, Arno Kutner, told me about a lawyer named Gerry Spence who had a series of how to video on jury selection and opening statement. I had never heard of him. Also as previously discussed, I desperately relied on his teachings in a case against Walt Disney World that was pivotal to my career. I watched the videos over and over. I felt an immediate connection to the clear, kind blue eyes of the man in the fringe jacket. I took notes and plagiarized his *voir dire* almost verbatim. I do remember calling Arno late at night before the closing argument, panicked that I did not know what to do. At that time, Spence had not yet issued a closing argument video. Arno spent several hours on the phone walking me through it.

Fortunately for me, and more so for my clients, the Orlando jury returned a verdict in their favor. The verdict remains, outside of the birth of my children, one of the greatest moments of my life.

I wrote Gerry Spence a letter, attaching a copy of the verdict. I told him how much I appreciated the videos, telling him that the verdict was as much his as mine. I never expected a reply, but a week later a hand written note arrived from him, saying how proud he was of me and that he hopes one day we could meet.

I wrote back (this predates e-mail) and Spence wrote back to me, saying he would be in Florida speaking at a law school and that I should stop by. Months passed, and I became increasingly excited about meeting him. In the meantime, I read a few of his books and learned that he had started a program to teach lawyers called the Trial Lawyers College.

When I finally met him, I had trouble restraining myself from crying. We spoke about my desire to represent people, the trial against Disney and how I had no formal training or teacher on how to be a trial lawyer. A week later, an application arrived for the Trial Lawyers College.

I completed it in a few hours and mailed it back to Wyoming--Then waited. Months passed until I finally got a letter from Spence with the good news: I had been accepted. Fifty lawyers from around the country who were either civil plaintiff's lawyers or criminal defense lawyers were invited to spend a month at Spence's ranch and learn to be effective advocates for people from some of the greatest lawyers in America. If you represent businesses, insurance companies or the government, you need not apply.

I had only been married one year when I boarded the plane for Jackson, Wyoming. I had packed suits and ties and loafers with little tassels. Yes, I was raised in Wichita, Kansas, but Jackson, Wyoming--or more precisely Dubois, where Gerry's ranch is--makes Wichita seem like Paris by comparison.

Gerry's ranch is a four hour bus ride from the Jackson airport. When I got off the bus, I was taken to a large barn, where Gerry and his family had turned the horse stalls into dorm rooms and the top floor where hay was kept was made into a courtroom/class room.

I shared a small dorm room with a huge guy named Charlie Aburesk. Charlie had a long pony tail and a soft voice. He is Lebanese, but has lived amongst the Lakota people most of his life. Over the next thirty days, the fifty lawyers spent fifteen hours per day, tearing us inside out through a process called psychodrama. It is Gerry's use of this therapeutic process to make lawyers "real." Most lawyers become shellacked and devoid of authentic feelings by years of the process of being lawyers. It starts for most in law school and continues to get worse. We start calling cars "vehicles;" the word before becomes "prior;" after becomes "subsequent" and so on. What's worse is we make it difficult to form meaningful connections with our clients and jurors (who we once called, "people"). Spence's process is meant to allow lawyers the permission to feel and be real.

For some it works; others find it too "touchy feely." I loved it. And every morning, I would join Spence on a two hour hike up a mountain to talk about everything. A real friendship was created. We laughed and we cried.

Near the end of the month, Spence told me he was about to embark on a forty-five day nationwide book tour to promote his book on the OJ Simpson case. He asked me to join him as he went city to city in his small plane. At the time, I had been away from my wife, house, dog and law practice already nearly a month. The thought of being gone another forty-five days seemed rough, but the opportunity to see the country with Spence was too valuable to pass by.

We met a few weeks later in New York and I watched and learned how he lectured, gave media interviews and interacted with people. It was a very valuable experience. Some towns were more exciting than others, but by the time we reached Seattle (forty days later) I was ready to come home.

I later joined Spence on another book tour and hope that he will join me on the tour of this book. My time with Spence has in many ways made me not just the lawyer I am, but the person I am. I lecture often to lawyers and law students, and every speech is inspired by Spence's teaching. The writing of this book is inspired by Spence's teaching. Every time, I speak with a client or jury or judge, it's based in some part by what Spence has taught me. I love the man.

I also returned several times to the Trial Lawyers College as part of his faculty. It has been a few years since I have been there, but I urge anyone reading this who wants to learn how to be a real advocate for the people to attend one of the Trial Lawyers College seminars--and leave the tasseled loafers at home.

Book tour with Gary L. Spence. I introduced him in bookstores, law schools and book signings across the country on two national book tours.

15 FINAL THOUGHTS AND ONE MORE GOLDEN RULE

I have learned so much from the experience of owning my own law firm; the pain of it was well worth it, and if given the chance, I would do it all over again. Let me spare you some of the pain if I can. Here is a big secret: *your firm is not you.*

Yes, your name may be on the letterhead, pleadings, verdicts, and paychecks, but it's a business. It's just a thing. If a client leaves you or an employee quits, do not view it as a personal tragedy. It's just a business. Yes, it is hard for those of us who put our blood and breath into what we do, but it is not you or who you are any more than this book is me. You may read this book, think it is the greatest waste of paper in history, and throw it in the garbage. You can even tell me that by e-mailing me at aronfeld@aronfeld.com. I will not take it as a personal rejection. This book is not me, although the stories are certainly mine.

AND FINALLY, below is a checklist to refer to before hanging your shingle.

1. Set up a mentor network.
2. Hire a lawyer and determine what corporate entity is right for you.

3. Register your company name with the local business department.

4. Hire an accountant.

5. Incorporate and then get a federal tax ID number. Your banker will help you.

6. Find office space.

7. Get an IT guy.

8. Get a phone line with voicemail.

9. Get a copier, scanner, and fax machine.

10. Get a laptop that allows you to fax and e-mail wirelessly from anywhere.

11. Design a logo.

12. Set up a website.

13. Get business cards.

14. Set up a Facebook account.

15. Get a scheduler and start planning your days, weeks, and months. (Nothing is more depressing than looking at an empty calendar. Let's fill it up!)

I am so much more than the practice of law, a law firm, or the paper and pencils that fill my desk drawers—as are you. Please do not ever forget that. Now go fly solo and soar.

Spencer Aronfeld
Coral Gables
January, 14, 2011

To see photographs of the people and places mentioned in this book, and for updates and other materials, please visit our website: www. makeityourownlawfirm.com

Appendix:
SAMPLE PARTNERSHIP AGREEMENT

This Agreement is presented here with the caveat that it is not designed for any one jurisdiction. Before using this, or any other form, be sure to check on applicable laws where you are. We make no warranties whatsoever regarding the use of this form.

THIS PARTNERSHIP AGREEMENT is made this _____ day of _____ 2XXX , by and between John Doe ("Doe") and Mark Smith ("Smith").

THE Parties hereto seek to enter into a binding agreement for the formation and operation of a Law Firm Partnership to be known as, "Smith & Doe, P.A.," to be formed under the laws of the State of Florida.

NOW THEREFORE, in consideration of their mutual promises, covenants, and agreements, and the Explanatory Statement, and for other valuable consideration, the sufficiency and accuracy of which is hereby acknowledged, the parties hereto do hereby promise, covenant and agree as follows:

Definitions

Throughout this Partnership Agreement, and unless the context otherwise requires, the word or words set forth below within the quotation marks shall be deemed to mean the words which follow them:

1. "Agreement" - This Partnership Agreement.

2. "Bankruptcy" - The filing by a Partner of a petition commencing a voluntary case under the Bankruptcy Code; a general assignment by a Party for the benefit of creditors; an admission in writing by a Partner of his inability to pay his debts as they become due; the filing by a Partner of any petition or answer in any proceeding seeking for himself or consenting to, or acquiescing in, any insolvency, receivership, composition, readjustment, liquidation, dissolution, or similar relief under any present

or future statute, law or regulation, or the filing by a Partner of an answer or other pleading admitting or failing to deny, or to contest, the material allegations of the petition filed against him in any such proceeding; the seeking or consenting to, or acquiescence by a Partner in, the appointment of any trustee, receiver, or liquidator of him, or any part of his property; and the commencement against a Partner of an involuntary case under the Bankruptcy Code, or a proceeding under any receivership, composition, readjustment, liquidation, insolvency, dissolution or like law or statute, which case or proceeding is not dismissed or vacated within 60 days.

3. "Partner" - Each of the persons signatory hereto and any other person or persons who may subsequently be designated as a general partner of this partnership pursuant to the further terms of this Agreement.

4. "Partnership" - This general partnership.

5. "Partnership Interest" - The share of profits and surplus of a Partner.

6. "Partnership Rights" - The property rights of a Partner, which are comprised of a Partner's: (1) right in specific partnership property, (2) interest in the Partnership and (3) right to participate in the management thereof.

7. "Persons" - Individuals, partnership, corporations, unincorporated associations, trusts, estates and any other type of entity.

8. "Retirement" - The decision or determination of a Partner to no longer continue as a Partner, upon written notice to all of the other Partners.

Section 1. Name

The name of the Partnership shall be "Smith & Doe, PA."

Section 2. Principal Place of Business

The principal office and place of business of the Partnership (the "Office") shall be located at [specify address]. The Partnership shall have such other or additional offices as the Partners may, from time to time, determine in accordance with Section 8 of this Agreement.

Section 3. Business and Purpose

The business and purposes of the Partnership are to form and operate a Law Firm as defined and regulated by the State Bar and to authorize transactions in furtherance of that purpose.

Section 4. Term

The Partnership shall commence upon the date of this Agreement, as set forth above and shall continue indefinitely unless sooner terminated pursuant to the further provisions of this Agreement.

Section 5. Capital Contribution

5.1. The original capital contributions to the Partnership of each of the Partners shall be made concurrently with their respective execution, acknowledgement, sealing and delivery of this Agreement in the following dollar amounts set forth after their respective names:

Doe	$20,000.00
Smith	$20,000.00

5.2. An individual capital account shall be maintained for each Partner. The capital account of each Partner shall consist of his or her original capital contribution, increased by (a) additional capital contributions made by him or her, (b) his or her share of Partnership profits, and decreased by (i) distributions of such profits and capital to him or her, and (ii) his or her share of Partnership losses.

5.3. Except as specifically provided in this Agreement, or as otherwise provided by and in accordance with law to the extent such law is not inconsistent with this Agreement, no Partner shall have the right to withdraw or reduce his or her contributions to the capital of the Partnership.

Section 6. Profit and Loss

6.1. The percentages of Partnership Rights and Partnership Interest of each of the Partners shall be as follows:

Doe	50%
Smith	50%

6.2. Except as provided in Section 7.3. of this Agreement, for purposes of Sections 702 and 704 of the Internal Revenue Code of 1954, or the corresponding provisions of any future federal internal revenue law, or any similar tax law of any state or jurisdiction, the determination of each Partner's distributive share of all items of income, gain, loss, deduction, credit or allowance of the Partnership for any period or year shall be made in accordance with, and in proportion to, such Partner's percentage of Partnership Interest as it may then exist.

Section 7. Distribution of Profits

7.1. The net cash from operations of the Partnership shall be distributed at such times as may be determined by the Partners in accordance with Section 8 of this Agreement among the Partners in proportion to their respective percentages of Partnership Interest, provided, however, that no amount of net cash from operations shall be distributed during any fiscal year of the Partnership until after the Partnership has paid any required installment of the aggregate Purchase Price or Special Aggregate Purchase Price, as the case may be, provided in Section 19 hereof.

7.2. As used in this Section 7, the term "net cash from operations" shall mean:

7.2.1. The taxable income of the Partnership for federal income tax purposes as shown on the books of the Partnership, increased by (a) the amount of depreciation and amortization deductions taken in computing such taxable income and (b) any non-taxable income or receipts of the Partnership, and reduced by (i) payments upon the principal of any installment obligations, mortgages or deeds of trust respecting Partnership assets or of other Partnership debts, and (ii) such expenditures for capital improvements or replacements, such reserves for said improvements and replacements and such reserves for repairs and to meet anticipated expenses and for working capital as the Partners, in accordance with Section 8 of this Agreement, shall deem to be reasonably necessary in the efficient conduct of the business; plus

7.2.2. Any excess funds resulting from the placement, or excess of refinancing of, any mortgages or deeds of trust on Partnership Property or the encumbrancing or financing of such Property in any other manner; plus

7.2.3. Any other funds (including amounts previously set aside for reserves by the Partners, in accordance with Section 8 of this Agreement, to the extent the Partner, in accordance with Section 8 of this Agreement, no longer regards such reserves as reasonably necessary in the efficient conduct of the Partnership business) deemed available for the distribution by the Partners, in accordance with Section 8 of this Agreement.

7.2.4. In determining the amount of net cash from operations any negative balances in any category described in Section 7.2.1., 7.2.2. and 7.2.3. shall be netted against the positive balances in the other such categories. Cumulative negative or positive balances shall be carried forward.

7.3. In addition to the distributions pursuant to Section 7.1. of this Agreement, upon any sale, transfer or other disposition of any capital asset of the Partnership (hereinafter referred to as a "Disposition"), the proceeds of such Disposition shall first be applied to the payment or repayment of any selling or other expenses incurred in connection with the Disposition and to the payment of any indebtedness secured by the asset subject to the Disposition immediately prior thereto; all proceeds remaining thereafter (the "Net Proceeds") shall be retained by the Partnership or be distributed, at such time or times as shall be determined by the Partners in accordance with Section 8 of this Agreement to the Partners in proportion to their respective percentages of Partnership Interest; provided, however, that for purposes of Sections 702 and 704 of the Internal Revenue Code of 1954, or the corresponding provisions of any future federal internal revenue law, or any similar tax law of any state or jurisdiction, each Partner's distributive share of all items of income, gain, loss, deduction, credit or allowance in respect of any such Disposition shall be made and based upon such Partner's basis in such capital asset.

Section 8. Management of the Partnership Business

8.1. All decisions respecting the management, operation and control of the Partnership business and determination made in accordance with the provisions of this Agreement shall be made only by the unanimous vote or consent of all of the Partners.

8.2. Nothing herein contained shall be construed to constitute any Partner or the agent of another Partner, except as expressly provided herein, or in any manner to limit the Partnership to the carrying on of their own respective businesses or activities. Any of the Partners, or any agent, servant or employee of any of the Partners, may engage in and possess any interest in other businesses or ventures of every nature and description, independently or with other persons, whether or not, directly or indirectly, in competition with the business or purpose of the Partnership, and neither the Partnership nor any of the Partners shall have any rights, by virtue of this Agreement or otherwise, in and to such independent ventures or the income or profits derived therefrom, or any rights, duties or obligations in respect thereof.

8.3. The Partners shall devote to the conduct of the Partnership business so much of their respective time as may be reasonably necessary for the efficient operation of the Partnership business.

Section 9. Salaries

Unless otherwise agreed by the Partners in accordance with Section 8 of this Agreement, no Partner shall receive any salary for services rendered to or for the Partnership.

Section 10. Legal Title to Partnership Property

Legal title to the property of the Partnership shall be held in the name of or in such other name or manner as the Partners shall determine to be in the best interest of the Partnership. Without limiting the foregoing grant of authority, the Partners may arrange to have title taken and held in their own names or in the names of trustees, nominees or straw parties for the Partnership. It is expressly understood and agreed that the manner of holding title to property (or any part thereof) of the Partnership is solely for the convenience of the Partnership, and that all such property shall be treated as Partnership property subject to the terms of this Agreement.

Section 11. Banking

All revenue of the Partnership shall be deposited regularly in the Partnership savings and checking accounts at such bank or banks as shall be selected by the Partners in accordance with Section 8 of this Agreement, and the signatures of such Partners as shall be determined in accordance with Section 8 of this Agreement shall be honored for banking purposes, other than the extension of credit to, or the borrowing of money by or on behalf of, the Partnership.

Section 12. Fiscal Year, Audits

Accurate and complete books of account shall be kept by the Partners and entries promptly made therein of all of the transactions of the Partnership, and such books of account shall be open at all times to the inspection and examination of the Partners. The books shall be kept on the basis of accounting selected by the accountant regularly servicing the Partnership and the fiscal year of the Partnership shall be the calendar year. A compilation, review or audit of the Partnership, as shall be determined by the Partners in accordance with Section 8 of this Agreement, shall be made as of the closing of each fiscal year of the Partnership by the accountants who shall then be engaged by the Partnership.

Section 13. Transfer of Partnership Interest and Partnership Rights

Except as otherwise provided in Sections 14, 15 and 16 hereof, no Partner (hereinafter referred to as the "Offering Partner") shall, during the term of the Partnership, sell, hypothecate, pledge, assign or otherwise transfer with or without consideration (hereinafter collectively referred to as a "Transfer") any part or all of his Partnership Interest or Partnership Rights in the Partnership to any other person (a "Transferee"), without first offering (hereinafter referred to as the "Offer") that portion of his Partnership Interest and Partnership Rights in the Partnership subject to the contemplated transfer (hereinafter referred to as the "Offered Interest") first to the Partnership, and secondly, to the other Partners, at a purchase price (hereinafter referred to as the "Transfer Purchase Price") and in a manner as follows:

13.1. The Transfer Purchase Price shall be the Appraised Value (as defined in Section 18.1.)

13.1.1. The Offer shall be made by the Offering Partner first to the Partnership by written notice (hereinafter referred to as the "Offering Notice). Within twenty (20) days (hereinafter referred to as the "Partnership Notice"), whether or not the Partnership shall accept the Offer and shall purchase all but not less than all of the Offered Interest. If the Partnership accepts the Offer to purchase the Offered Interest, the Partnership Notice shall fix a closing date not more than twenty-five (25) days (hereinafter referred to as the "Partnership Closing Date") after the expiration of the Partnership Offer Period.

13.1.2. In the event the Partnership decides not to accept the Offer, the Offering Partner or the Partnership, at his or its election, shall, by written notice (hereinafter referred to as the "Remaining Partner Notice") given within that period (hereinafter referred to as the "Partner Offer Period") terminating ten (10) days after the expiration of the Partnership Offer Period, make the Offer of the Offered Interest to the other Partners, each of whom shall then have a period of twenty-five (25) days (the "Partner Acceptance Period") after the expiration of the Partner Offer Period within which to notify in writing the Offering Partner whether or not he intends to purchase all but not less than all of the Offered Interest. If two (2) or more Partners of the Partnership desire to accept the Offer to purchase the Offered Interest, then, in the absence of an agreement between them, such Partners shall have the right to purchase the Offered Interest in the proportion which their respective percentage of Partnership Interest in the Partnership bears to the percentage of Partnership Interest of all of the Partners who desire to accept the Offer. If the other Partners intend to accept the Offer and purchase the Offered Interest, the written notice required to be given by them shall fix a closing date not more than ten (10) days after the expiration of the Partner Acceptance Period (hereinafter referred to as the "Partner Closing Date").

13.2. The aggregate dollar amount of the Transfer Purchase Price shall be payable in cash on the Partnership closing date or on the Partner Closing date, as the case may be, unless the Partnership or the purchasing Partners shall elect prior to or on the Partnership Closing Date or the Partner Closing Date, as the case may be, to purchase such Offered Interest in installments pursuant to the provisions of Section 19 hereof.

13.3. If the Partnership or the other Partners fail to accept the Offer or, if the Offer is accepted by the Partnership or the other Partners and the Partnership or the other Partners fail to purchase all of the Offered Interest at the Transfer Purchase Price within the time and in the manner specified in this Section 13, then the Offering Partner shall be free, for a period (hereinafter referred to as the "Free Transfer Period") of sixty (60) days from the occurrence of such failure, to transfer the Offered Interest to a Transferee; subject only to any additional restrictions on such Transfer that may be imposed by this Agreement or any other agreement. Any such Transferee, upon acquiring the Offered Interest, shall automatically be bound by the terms of this Agreement and shall be required to join in, execute, acknowledge, seal and deliver a copy of this Agreement as a result of which he shall become an additional party hereto. If the Offering Partner shall not transfer the Offered Interest within the Free Transfer Period, his right to transfer the Offered Interest free of the foregoing restrictions shall thereupon cease and terminate.

13.4. No transfer made pursuant to this Section 13 shall dissolve or terminate the Partnership or cause the Partnership to be wound-up, but instead, the business of the Partnership shall be continued as if such Transfer had not occurred.

Section 14. Buy Sell Agreement

The parties agree to enter into a buy/sell agreement to effect purchase of the deceased partner's share upon such partner's death, to be funded by life insurance policies.

Section 15. Purchase Upon Bankruptcy or Retirement.

15.1. Upon the Bankruptcy or Retirement from the Partnership of any Partner (the "Withdrawing Partner"), the Partnership shall neither be terminated nor wound-up, but, instead, the business of the Partnership shall be continued as if such Bankruptcy or Retirement, as the case may be, had not occurred, and the Partnership shall purchase and the Withdrawing Partner shall sell all of the Partnership Interest and Partnership Rights (the "Withdrawing Partner's Interest") owned by the Withdrawing Partner in the Partnership on the date of such Bankruptcy or retirement (the "Withdrawal Date"). The Partnership shall, by written notice addressed to the Withdrawing Partner or to the legal representative of a bankrupt Partner, fix a closing date for such purchase which shall be not less than seventy-five (75) days after the Withdrawal Date. The Withdrawing Partner's Interest shall be purchased by the Partnership on such closing date at a price (the "Withdrawing Purchase Price") which shall be the Appraised Value (as defined in Section 18.1 of this Agreement.)

15.2. The aggregate dollar amount of the Withdrawing Purchase Price shall be payable in cash on the closing date, unless the Partnership shall elect prior to or on the closing date to purchase the Withdrawing Partner's Interest in installments as provided in Section 19 of this Agreement.

Section 16. Certain Further Events Giving Rights to Purchase Option.

16.1. In the event that any Partner (the "Defaulting Partner"):

16.1.1. Shall have filed against him any tax lien respecting all or substantially all of his property and such tax lien shall not be discharged, removed or bonded within sixty (60) days of the date on which it was filed; or

16.1.2. Shall subject his Partnership Interest or Partnership Rights or any part thereof or interest therein to a charging order entered by any court of competent jurisdiction; then, immediately upon the occurrence of either of said events (the "Occurrence Date"), the Partnership shall have the right and option, exercisable by written notice to the Defaulting Partner, within thirty (30) days of the Occurrence Date, to purchase from the Defaulting Partner, who shall sell to the Partnership, all of the Partnership Interest and Partnership Rights (the "Defaulting Partner's Interest) owned by the Defaulting Partner in the Partnership on the Occurrence Date. The Partnership shall, by written notice delivered to the Defaulting Partner or his successors, fix a closing date for such purchase which shall be not less than forty (40) days after the Occurrence Date, but in no event longer than seventy-five (75) days after the Occurrence Date. The Defaulting Partner's Interest shall be purchased by the Partnership on such closing date at a price (the "Defaulting Partner's Purchase Price") which shall be the Appraised Value (as defined in Section 18.1 of this Agreement).

16.2. The aggregate dollar amount of the Defaulting Partner's Purchase Price shall be payable in cash on the closing date, unless the Partnership shall elect prior to or on the closing date to purchase the Defaulting Partner's Interest in installments as provided in Section 19 of this Agreement.

Section 17. Certain Tax Aspects Incident to Transactions Contemplated by this Agreement.

It is the intention of the parties that the Transfer Purchase Price, the Decedent Purchase Price, the Withdrawing Purchase Price and the Defaulting Partner's Purchase Price shall constitute and be considered as made in exchange for the interest of the retired Partner in partnership property, including good will, within the meaning of Section 736(b) of the Internal Revenue Code of 1954, as amended.

Section 18. The Appraised Value.

18.1. The term "Appraised Value" as used in this Agreement shall be the dollar amount equal to the product obtained by multiplying (a) the percentage of Partnership Interest and Partnership Rights owned by a Partner by (b) the Fair Market Value of the Partnership's assets, as determined in accordance with Section 18.2.

18.2. The Fair Market Value of the Partnership's assets shall be determined in the following manner:

18.2.1. Within thirty (30) days of the date of the Offering Notice, date of the death of a Decedent, the Withdrawal Date or the Occurrence Date, as the case may be, the remaining Partners shall select an appraiser (the "Partnership Appraiser") to determine the Fair Market Value of the Partnership's assets, and the Partnership Appraiser shall submit his determination thereof within thirty (30) days after the date of his selection (the "Appraisal Due Date").

18.2.2. If the appraisal made by Partnership Appraiser is unsatisfactory to the Offering Partner, the personal representatives of the Decedent or Heir, the Withdrawing Partner or the Defaulting Partner, as the case may be, then within fifteen (15) days after the date of the Appraisal Due Date, the Offering Partner, the personal representatives of the Decedent or Heir, the Withdrawing Partner or the Defaulting Partner, as the case may be, shall select an appraiser (the "Partner's Appraiser") to determine the Fair Market Value of the Partnership's assets, and such appraiser shall submit his determination thereof within thirty (30) days after the date of his selection.

18.2.3. If the appraisal made by the Partner's Appraiser is unsatisfactory to the remaining Partners, then the Partnership Appraiser and the Partner's Appraiser shall select a third appraiser (the "Appraiser") to determine the Fair Market Value of the Partnership's assets and such Appraiser shall submit his determination thereof within thirty (30) days after the date of his selection. The Appraiser's determination thereof shall be binding upon the Partnership, the remaining Partners and the Offering Partner, the personal representatives of the Decedent or Heir, the Withdrawing Partner or the Defaulting Partner, as the case may be.

18.3. Any and all appraisers selected in accordance with the provisions of this Section 18 shall be [specify city] area appraisers, who shall conduct appraisals provided for in this Section 18 in accordance with generally accepted appraising standards. Any and all costs incurred in connection with any of the appraisals provided for in this Section 18 shall be borne equally by the remaining Partners, and the Offering partner, the personal representatives of the Decedent or Heir, the Withdrawing or the Defaulting Partner, as the case may be.

Section 19. Installment Payments.

19.1. In the event that there shall be an election pursuant to the provisions of Sections 13.2, 14.2, 15.2 or 16.2 hereof to purchase (the Partner or the Partnership so purchasing shall be hereinafter, where appropriate, referred to as the "purchasing person", the Offering Partner's interest, the Decedent's Interest, the Withdrawing Partner's Interest or the Defaulting Partner's Interest, as the case may be (hereinafter where appropriate, referred to as the "Interest"), on an installment basis, then the terms and conditions of such installment purchase shall be as set forth in Section 19.1.1 and Section 19.1.2 in the case of an election pursuant to Section 13.2 or Section 14.2 and as set forth in Section 19.1.2 and Section 19.1.3 in the case of an election pursuant to Section 15.2 or Section 16.2 hereof.

19.1.1. Twenty-nine percent (29%) of the aggregate purchase price due for such Interest (hereinafter, where appropriate, referred to as the "Aggregate Purchase Price') shall be paid on the closing date; and

19.1.2. The remainder of the Aggregate Purchase Price shall be paid in three (3) equal consecutive annual installments on each anniversary of the closing date over a period, beginning with the year following the calendar year in which the sale occurred (hereinafter referred to as the "Installment Payment Period").

19.1.3. Twenty-nine percent (29%) of the aggregate purchase price due for such Interest (hereinafter, where appropriate, referred to as the "Special Aggregate Purchase Price") shall be paid on the closing date; and

19.1.4. The remainder of the Special Aggregate Purchase Price shall be paid in three (3) equal consecutive annual installments on each anniversary of the closing date over a period, beginning with the year following the calendar year in which the date occurred (hereinafter referred to as the "Special Installment Payment Period").

19.1.5. Anything contained in this Section 19 to the contrary notwithstanding, the entire unpaid balance of the Aggregate Purchase Price and Special Aggregate Purchase Price shall become immediately due and payable upon the sale, exchange, transfer or other disposition of all or substantially all of the Property or assets of the Partnership.

19.1.6. The purchasing person shall pay simple interest at a rate shall be equal to the prime rate of interest then being charged by CitiBank, N.A., New York City, New York, to its highest credit-rated corporate borrowers on short term unsecured commercial borrowings on the unpaid balance of the Aggregate Purchase Price of Special Aggregate Purchase Price on each anniversary of the closing date during the Installment Payment Period or Special Installment Payment Period, as the case may be.

19.2. So long as any part of the Aggregate Purchase Price or Special Aggregate Purchase Price remains unpaid, the Partners shall permit the Offering Partner, the personal representatives of the Decedent or the Heir, the Withdrawing Partner (or the legal representative of the Withdrawing Partner in the event of the bankruptcy of the Withdrawing Partner) or the Defaulting Partner, as the case may be, and the attorneys and accountants of each of the foregoing persons, to examine the books and records of the Partnership and its business following the event that shall have given rise to the election referred to in Section 19.1 hereof during regular business hours from time to time upon reasonable prior notice and to receive copies of the annual accounting reports and tax returns of the Partnership.

Section 20. Delivery of Evidence of Interest

On the closing date, upon payment of the Aggregate Purchase Price for the purchase of the Interest hereunder or, if payment is to be made in installments pursuant to the provisions of Section 19 hereof, upon the first payment, the Offering Partner, the Withdrawing Partner, the personal representative of the Withdrawing Partner (in the event of the bankruptcy of the Withdrawing Partner) or the Defaulting Partner, as the case may be, shall execute, acknowledge, seal and deliver to the purchasing person such instrument or instruments of transfer to evidence the purchase of the Interest (the "Instrument of Transfer") that shall be reasonably requested by counsel to the purchasing person in form and substance; reasonably satisfactory to such counsel. If a tender of the Aggregate Purchase Price or Special Aggregate Purchase Price or, if payment is to be made in installments pursuant to the provisions of Section 19.1 hereof, the tender of the first payment thereof, shall be refused, or if the Instrument of Transfer shall not be delivered contemporaneously with the tender of the Aggregate Purchase Price or Special Aggregate Purchase Price or of the first payment thereof, as aforesaid, then the purchasing person shall be appointed, and the same is hereby irrevocably constituted and appointed the attorney-in-fact with full power and authority to execute, acknowledge, seal and deliver the Instrument of Transfer.

Section 21. Family Members.

For purposes of this Agreement, members of the "immediate family" of a Partner are hereby defined to be such person's spouse or children.

Section 22. Notices.

Any and all notices, offers, acceptances, requests, certifications and consents provided for in this Agreement shall be in writing and shall be given and be deemed to have been given when personally delivered against a signed receipt or mailed by registered or certified mail, return receipt requested, to the last address which the addressee has given to the Partnership. The address of each partner is set under his signature at the end of this Agreement, and each partner agrees to notify the Partnership of any change of address. The address of the Partnership shall be its principal office.

Section 23. Governing Law.

It is the intent of the parties hereto that all questions with respect to the construction of this Agreement and the rights, duties, obligations and liabilities of the parties shall be determined in accordance with the applicable provisions of the laws of the State of [specify].

Section 24. Miscellaneous Provisions.

24.1. This Agreement shall be binding upon, and inure to the benefit of, all parties hereto, their personal and legal representatives, guardians, successors, and their assigns to the extent, but only to the extent, that assignment is provided for in accordance with, and permitted by, the provisions of this Agreement.

24.2. Nothing herein contained shall be construed to limit in any manner the Partners, or their respective agents, servants, and employees, in carrying on their own respective businesses or activities.

24.3. The Partners agree that they and each of them will take whatever action or actions as are deemed by counsel to the Partnership to be reasonably necessary or desirable from time to time to effectuate the provisions of intent of this Agreement, and to that end, the Partners agree that they will execute, acknowledge, seal and deliver any further instruments or documents which may be necessary to give force and effect to this Agreement or any of the provisions hereof, or to carry out the intent of this Agreement, or any of the provisions hereof.

24.4. Throughout this Agreement, where such meanings would be appropriate: (a) the masculine gender shall be deemed to include the feminine and the neuter and vice-versa, and (b) the singular shall be deemed to include the plural, and vice-versa. The headings herein are inserted only as a matter of convenience and reference, and in no way define, limit or describe the scope of this Agreement, or the intent of any provisions thereof.

24.5. This Agreement and exhibits attached hereto set forth all (and are intended by all parties hereto to be an integration of all) of the promises, agreements, conditions, understandings, warranties and representations, oral or written, express or implied, among them other than as set forth herein.

24.6. Nothing contained in this Agreement shall be construed as requiring the commission of any act contrary to law. In the event there is any conflict between any provision of this Agreement and any statute, law, ordinance or regulation contrary to which the Partners have no legal right to contract, the later shall prevail, but in such event the provisions of this Agreement thus affected shall be curtailed and limited only to the extent necessary to conform with said requirement of law. In the event that any part, article, section, paragraph or clause of this Agreement shall be held to be indefinite, invalid or otherwise unenforceable, the entire Agreement shall not fail on account thereof, and the balance of this Agreement shall continue in full force and effect.

24.7. Each married party to this Agreement agrees to obtain the consent and approval of his or her spouse, to all the terms and provisions of this Agreement; provided, however, that such execution shall be for the sole purpose of acknowledging such spousal consent and approval, as aforesaid, and nothing contained in this Section 24.7 shall be deemed to have constituted any such spouse a Partner in the Partnership.

24.8. Each partner agrees to insert in his Will or to execute a Codicil thereto directing and authorizing his personal representatives to fulfill and comply with the provisions hereof and to sell and transfer his percentage of Partnership Interest and Partnership Rights in accordance herewith.

24.9. The Partnership shall have the right to make application for, take out and maintain in effect such policies of life insurance on the lives of any or all of the Partners, whenever and in such amounts as the Partners shall determine in accordance with Section 8 of this Agreement. Each Partner shall exert his best efforts and fully assist and cooperate with the Partnership in obtaining any such policies of life insurance.

IN WITNESS WHEREOF, the parties hereunto set their hands and seals and acknowledged this Agreement as of the date first above written.

_____

Witness

_____   _____

JOHN DOE   DATE

_____

Witness

_____   _____

MARK SMITH   DATE

FLORIDA INTERNATIONAL UNIVERSITY
Miami's public research university

College of Law   Office of the Dean

July 14, 2009

To whom it may concern:

I am a professor at the Florida International University School of Law who served until two weeks ago as its Founding Dean during eight and a half years. I have been a law professor at five law schools over the past 43 years having served as dean at three of them. I know legal education and I know the market for law school graduates.

I have usually counseled law students against planning to go into solo practice early in their careers because I have believed that early mentoring is important to a lawyer realizing his or her potential. Despite that advice, whether for economic reasons of simply personal choice, many graduates have chosen solo practice. I regret that they did not have a guide available like the one proposed by Attorney Spencer Aronfeld to help them in making their choice and then in building a career of competency and professionalism after they chose solo practice.

I have known Spencer as a respected practitioner in Miami and as one who has lectured to our FIU law students on the subject of whether to enter into solo practice and how to carry off that choice successfully. As the national economy has declined, so has the market of jobs for new lawyers in both the public and private sectors. In the next five years, I predict that we will see more and more young lawyers choosing solo practice as a bottleneck develops at the entry points to the legal profession, even as the economy recovers.

Two consequences of this pattern will be a need for a book of the kind Spencer Aronfeld is proposing and a need for courses in law schools to provide law students the preparation they will need to enter solo practice. I believe that the market for Spencer's book and others like it will be substantial. Spencer has such passion for this subject, having thought extensively about it and lectured on it at multiple law schools, that it seems probable that his book will gain good portion of that market.

I have confidence in Spencer Aronfeld. I am pleased to be supportive of him and his plan for this book.

Sincerely,

Leonard P. Strickman
Professor
Founding Dean Emeritus

UNIVERSITY OF Miami

SCHOOL OF LAW

July 6, 2009

To Whom it May Concern:

I am the Assistant Dean of Career Development at the University of Miami School of Law and have known Spencer Aronfeld for approximately 12 years. Spencer is a dedicated, hard-working, generous and exceptional attorney.

Spencer obtained his Juris Doctor degree from the University of Miami School of Law in 1991. Upon graduation, unlike many law school graduates who commenced their legal careers with law firms, government or public interest organizations, Spencer decided to open his own law firm. Since 1991, Spencer has successfully run his own law practice and has returned to our law school to furnish our students with valuable information regarding the practicalities of being a sole practitioner and the basics of opening up one's own law office immediately after law school.

Spencer has generously shared his time, knowledge and expertise with our students for the past 18 years. Each year, Spencer visits our campus to present his *Flying Solo* presentation to our students. Over the years, we have received great feedback from students who have attended his program, as well as those he has mentored. His presentation is vital to those students interested in starting their own practices. During a typical presentation, Spencer shares his experiences and advice on the following:

- how students can prepare for going solo while still in law school;
- how to develop clients;
- how to effectively utilize office space;
- how to develop a marketing plan;
- how to ethics and professionalism should be a part of every aspect of your practice;
- how to finance the firm's first cases; and
- how to partner with classmates or colleagues whose strengths counter one's weaknesses.

I was so pleased when Spencer told me that he was writing a book about starting one's own firm. I can't tell you what a valuable tool this book will be to recent graduates and experienced attorneys looking to open their shops, especially in today's legal marketplace.

If you have any questions about Spencer or require further information about his annual presentations, please let me know.

Sincerely,

Marcelyn R. Cox
Assistant Dean

One way to promote my firm and to do something for
the community at the same time is my sponsorship of the
City of Coral Gables annual Menorah Lighting.

MIAMILAW

University of Miami School of Law

The Mass Torts Litigation Society and
the Environmental Law Society
Presents

Spencer Aronfeld

As he speaks on CHINESE DRYWALL, the latest mass
tort litigation that is sweeping the nation.

Mr Aronfeld has been appointed a member of the Plaintiff's Steering committee
on Chinese Drywall. He has also been featured on the Today Show and other
National TV shows and is admitted to practice before the U.S. Supreme Court.

This is sure to be an exciting event you don't want to miss!!

Thursday, March 11th
Room E352 at 12:30 p.m.
Lunch will be provided.

For more information on Spencer Aronfeld: http://www.aronfeld.com/

This is an example of how I try to simultaneously promote
my practice and inform the community.

A good way to promote your law firm and to do good at the same
time is through community service. Lawyers to the Rescue is a
humanitarian not-for-profit foundation founded by my wife Dina
and me in 2010. Its aim is to improve lawyers' reputations by doing
good for people. Visit the site: www.lawyerstotherescue.com

Manage every stage of an auto injury case to your client's advantage.

GAINING THE BEST SETTLEMENT IN AUTO INJURY CASES

Miami, Florida
July 29, 2008

PRESENTED BY

Spencer M. Aronfeld
Aronfeld Trial Lawyers

Robert Coulombe Jr.
Clark, Robb, Mason, Coulombe, Buschman, and Cecere

Michael Shelley
Alvarez, Sambol, Winthrop, & Madson, P.A.

CONTINUING EDUCATION

CLE - 7.0
See inside for details!

Register Today!
800-930-6182 OR
www.nbi-sems.com

NBI NATIONAL BUSINESS INSTITUTE

Now Offering TELECONFERENCES

Speaking at seminars is another way to get the word out in the community about you and your law firm.

Keeping a watchful eye over my practice is a portrait of my
grandfather Samuel Aronfeld. While I never had the privilege of
knowing him, I refer to him as the firm's founding partner.

LaVergne, TN USA
23 March 2011

221377LV00002B/2/P